IMAGES
of America

OCALA

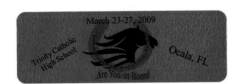

D1452019

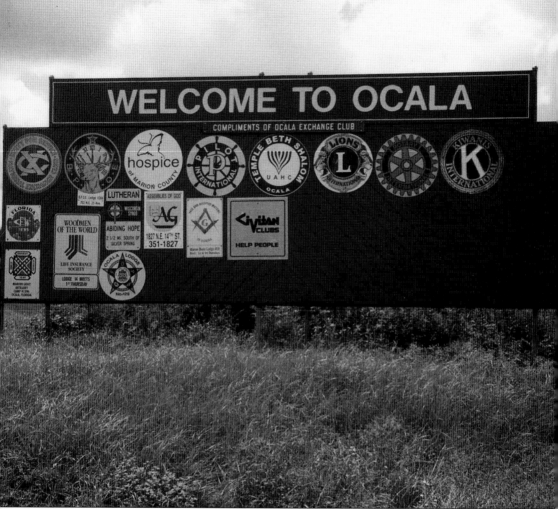

Visitors to the All-America city will find a warm welcome from a number of civic-minded organizations. (Kevin M. McCarthy.)

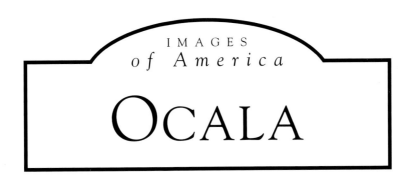

IMAGES
of America

OCALA

Kevin M. McCarthy and Ernest Jernigan

ARCADIA
PUBLISHING

CONTENTS

ACKNOWLEDGMENTS

Numerous people helped by providing pictures or caption material or both. Special thanks go to David Cook, Jay McKenzie, the Ernest Jernigan family, and the *Star-Banner*, which over the decades has presented valuable information. The following helped significantly: Sonny Allen, Peggy Cash, David Clements, Maureen Donovan, Jim Jernigan, Holly Lang, Katie Mulhearn, and Joe Wallace. We dedicate this book to our wives, Karelisa Hartigan and Fay Jernigan.

INTRODUCTION

Ocala, the biggest city of Marion County and its county seat, takes its name from an Indian name meaning "water's edge," probably referring to the location of an ancient settlement near Ocklawaha River. It was the early site of Fort King, the 1830s fort where the Second Seminole War was precipitated when Indians ambushed and killed the local federal officer in 1835. Ocala was also a popular destination for visitors traveling the Ocklawaha River from Jacksonville via the St. Johns River in the 19th century. In the 1890s, when phosphate was discovered nearby, local entrepreneurs promoted the town's central position in Florida as a reason for making it the state capital, but Tallahassee retained that honor. The phosphate in the soil enriched it to such an extent that many horse farms were established in the area, adding much to the economic well being of Ocala.

Ocala has been particularly important in the politics of the state, beginning with its hosting of the national convention of Farmers Alliance in 1890. Additionally, the city and surrounding area have given the state three governors and several lieutenant governors, as well as a number of African-American leaders such as former Secretary of the State of Florida Jesse J. McCrary Jr.

In 1995, the city was named an All-America City, a rare honor that few cities achieve. Those who live in Ocala were probably not too surprised at such an honor. The city, after all, has much going for it. Set midway between the Atlantic Ocean on the east and the Gulf of Mexico on the west, the town is provided with some protection from hurricanes, but its residents also enjoy easy access to boating, fishing, and swimming on both coasts. Ocala's latitude is such that it experiences a change of seasons but does not have the high heat of South Florida or the cold weather of the North. Nearby Silver and Juniper Springs offer welcome facilities for recreational swimming, canoeing, camping, and boating. This, as well as Ocala's proximity to many lakes, rivers, parks, and the Ocala National Forest (350,000 acres that make up the southernmost national forest in the continental United States) gives its residents no excuse to stay indoors. These attractions, the community's good educational facilities (especially Central Florida Community College), and the closeness of the University of Florida have enticed thousands of new residents to the area. Finally, Ocala's cross-section of people from various backgrounds, races, cultures, and languages give the city a cosmopolitan atmosphere that may surprise newcomers.

Today, Ocala boasts about 50,000 residents, with another 50,000 living just outside the city limits; Marion County has about 250,000. The city's prospects for the future are promising because of enlightened leadership, a forward-thinking newspaper, and a concern on the part of the residents to plan for the steady growth that will surely come in the 21st century.

One

BEFORE 1900

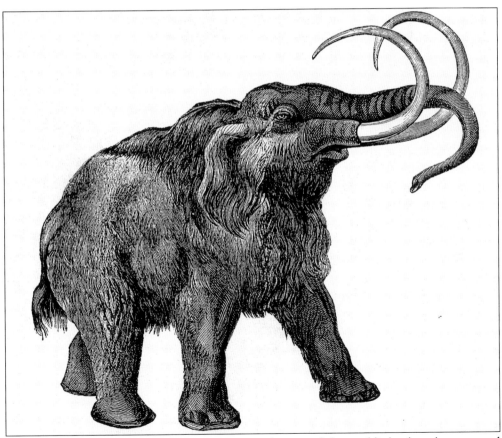

Thousands of years ago, when the ice ages caused many of the world's lands to be separated because much of the earth's water was frozen in glaciers, hunters crossed the Bering Strait from Asia to America in search of large animals such as the mastodon and mammoth. Around 12,000 years ago, some of those people reached Florida. (Dover Pictorial Archive Series.)

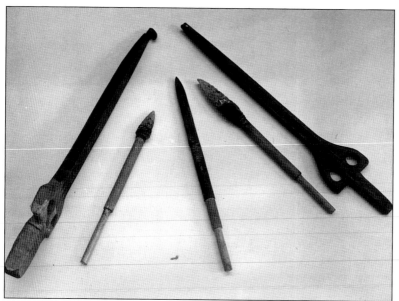

Early Native Americans used weapons like these to hunt animals. Archaeologists have found such weapons in rivers and springs throughout Florida. When the large animals died out, Native Americans had to adapt to fishing and farming to survive. (Florida State Archives)

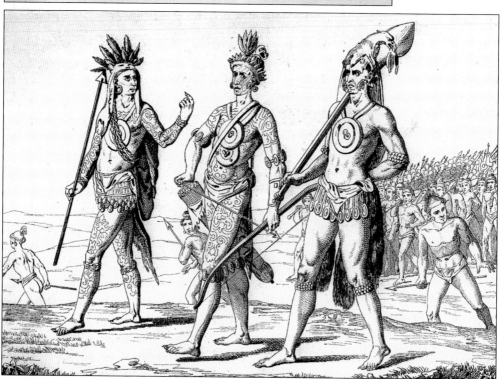

The Timucua Indians (pronounced "ti MOO kwa") were one of the largest groups of Native Americans in Florida (including the present-day Marion County) in the 16th century, when the Spanish first arrived. Remains of the bones of Native Americans, probably the Timucua, from between the years 500 B.C. and A.D. 1565 have been found in the Ocala National Forest. The Native American Graves Protection and Repatriation Act of 1996 requires that Native American remains, funeral, and sacred objects must be given back to descendants for reburial. (Florida State Archives.)

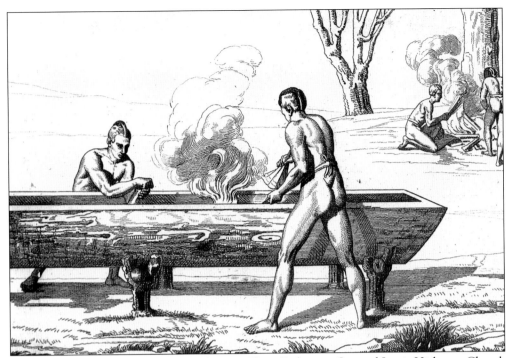

Two important historians of this Ocala area, Eloise Robinson Ott and Louis Hickman Chazal, pointed out that the slogan for the county, "The Kingdom of the Sun," goes back to the Timucua practice of worshiping the sun with ceremonial offerings. The picture above shows the Timucua making a canoe by burning the inside of a large log. (Florida State Archives.)

The Timucua included smaller divisions such as the Ocale and Potano in what is now Marion County. Several hundred villages were in the Timucua territory, and some of those villages had as many as 200 houses. Those houses were usually round, wooden huts covered with palm fronds and mud, which kept them cool in the summer and warm in the winter. (Florida State Archives.)

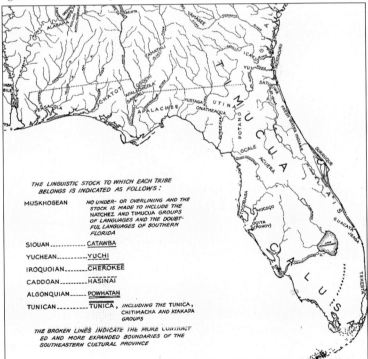

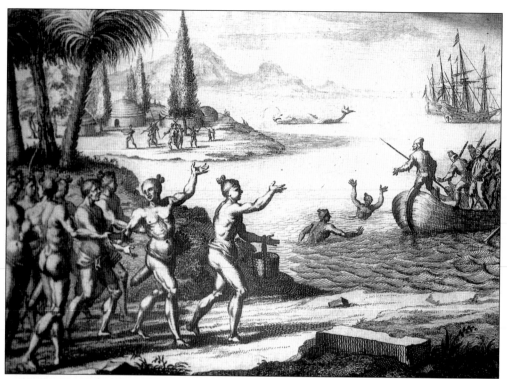

When Native Americans met Europeans for the first time in the early 16th century, both sides had much difficulty in understanding each other's languages. Native Americans in Florida spoke several languages, none of them Spanish. The picture above shows the Native Americans enthusiastically welcoming the Europeans, but that enthusiasm soon turned to hostility when the Europeans tried to make the Native Americans slaves and manual laborers. (Florida State Archives.)

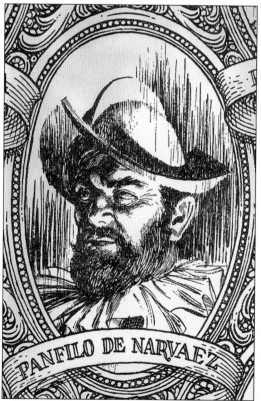

PANFILO DE NARVAEZ

Ponce de Leon was one of the first European explorers to come to Florida (1513), as was Panfilo de Narvez (pictured at left), who arrived in 1528 and led some 300 men up the peninsula from Tampa Bay to present-day Tallahassee, passing in or near modern Marion County. Attacks by the Native Americans, the bugs, heat, and swamps made such journeys very difficult. (Florida State Archives.)

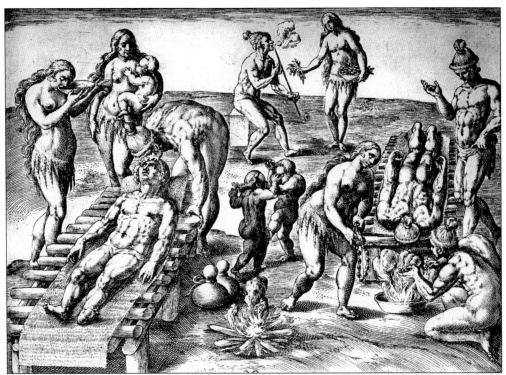

When European explorers began arriving in Florida in the early 1500s, around 250,000 Native Americans lived on the peninsula. Over the next 200 years, those Native Americans died from battles and the diseases that the Europeans brought with them, diseases to which they had no immunity. (Florida State Archives.)

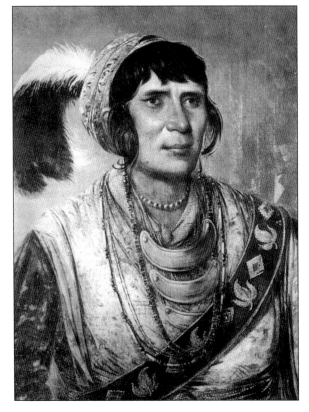

Osceola (1804–1838), a leader of the Seminole Indians, was responsible for the killing of General Thompson in 1835 at Fort King, which is today within the city limits of Ocala. The killing was one of the major causes of Florida's Second Seminole War (1835–1842). The soldiers' quarters at Fort King were later used as Marion County's first courthouse. (Florida State Archives.)

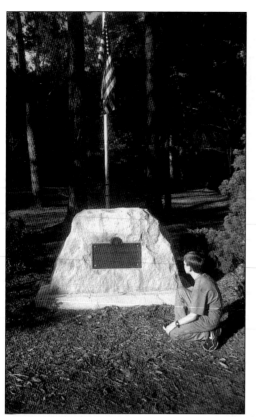

A burial marker at the former location of Fort King in Ocala commemorates the many federal troops killed there. The fort, built around 1827 to protect white settlers from the Native Americans in the area, honored Col. William King, whom Gen. Andrew Jackson had appointed as the civil and military governor of the provisional government of West Florida. (Kevin M. McCarthy.)

The Seminole woman below cooks over an open fire similar to the way her ancestors did in many parts of Florida. The Seminoles, who were originally Creek Indians living in Alabama and Georgia, migrated south to Florida in the 18th century to seek new lands where they could farm, hunt, and fish. Their name comes from a Creek phrase, "isti simanole," which was the Creek pronunciation of the Spanish "cimarrone," a word meaning "runaway," "untamed." (Florida State Archives.)

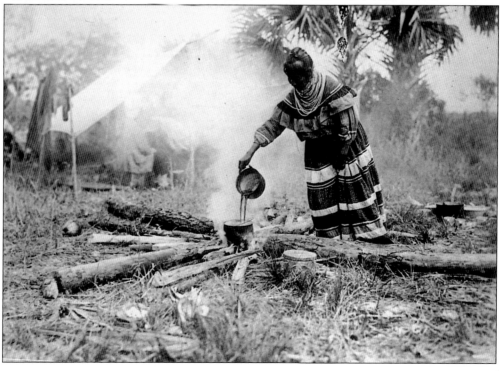

Seminoles, who still wear colorful, patchwork clothes at their various settlements throughout Florida, have prospered in the past hundred years. Today they are involved in successful businesses around the state, including the manufacture of airplanes in South Florida by the Micco Aircraft Company. The word "Micco" comes from a Seminole Indian word meaning "leader" or "superior one." (Florida State Archives.)

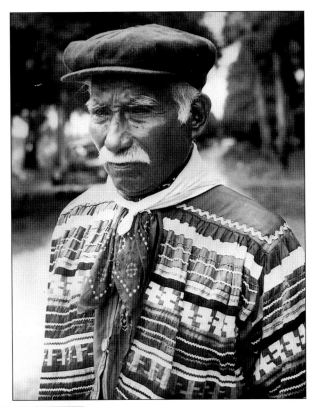

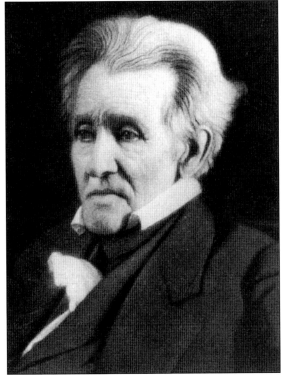

Andrew Jackson, who would later receive Florida from Spain on behalf of the American people and still later become President of the United States, defeated the Native Americans in Florida and expelled most of them from the state. (Florida State Archives.)

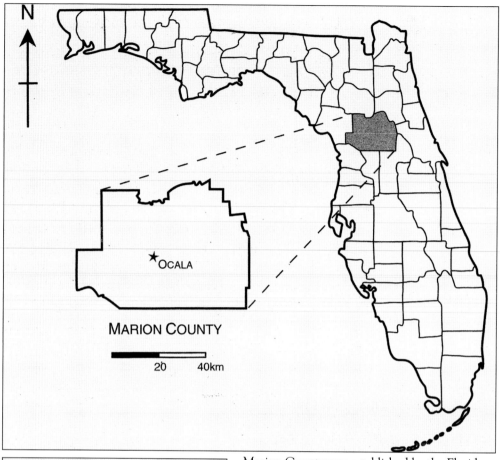

MARION COUNTY

★OCALA

20   40km

Marion County was established by the Florida Territorial Legislature in 1844 after many settlers had moved into the area to take advantage of the Armed Occupation Act of 1842, which was designed to lure settlers to the newly opened areas of Central Florida. Marion County's name honored Gen. Francis Marion, a Revolutionary War hero from South Carolina. Ocala was established in 1846.

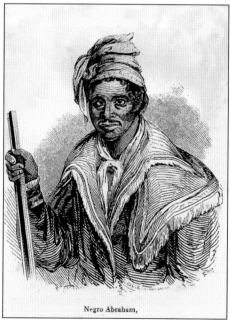

Negro Abraham,

Slaves who escaped from plantations in the Carolinas and Georgia sometimes fled to Florida where they found refuge with the Seminoles. These former slaves, sometimes called Black Seminoles, acted as interpreters between whites and Native Americans. One such Black Seminole was "Negro Abraham," a man associated with Chief Micanopy, who lived in what later became Marion County. (Florida State Archives.)

White plantation owners placed ads, like this one that ran in the *Jacksonville Courier* on April 26, 1835, in newspapers throughout Florida in an attempt to get their runaway slaves returned. (Florida State Archives.)

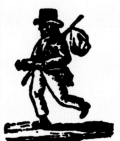

TEN DOLLARS REWARD.

RAN AWAY from the subscriber, a *Negro man* named *Charles*, and a *Negro woman* named *Dorcas*. The man is about forty years old, and the woman thirty-eight. The man is very black—about five feet nine inches in height,—with the African marks on his face of his native country. The woman is about five feet nine inches, and rather thick set. Any person returning them shall receive the above reward.   **HENRY W. MAXEY.**

Cedar Point, March 4.   1w10

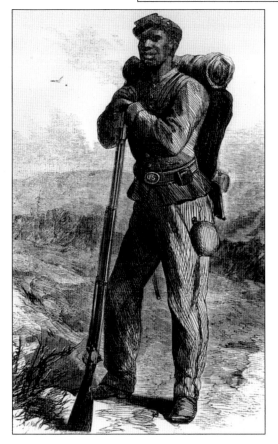

During the Civil War, Florida only had about 140,000 residents, close to half of whom were African American. Very few battles were fought in Florida during that war, but escaped slaves, like the man pictured here, served on the Union side and engaged Southern soldiers in battles like the one at Olustee in northern Florida in 1864. (Florida State Archives.)

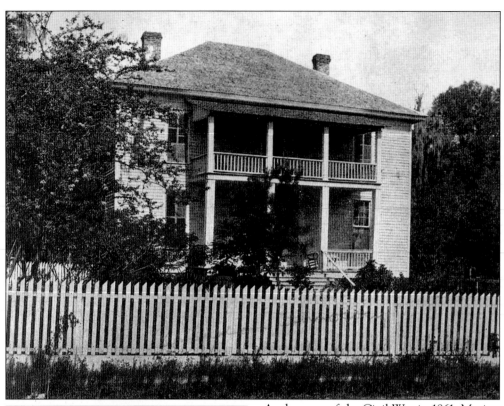

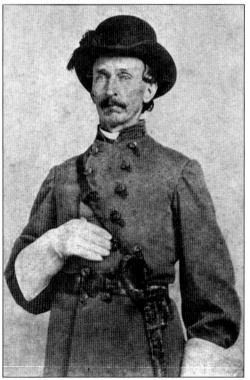

At the start of the Civil War in 1861, Marion County had fewer than 9,000 residents, with about 1,200 living in Ocala. Because 90 percent of those eligible to fight in the war did so, the women left behind ran the area's farms and plantations. The colonial home pictured above belonged to John Martin, the last living member of the Confederate Congress. Each year the Annual Ocklawaha River Raid reenacts the only Civil War battle fought in Marion County. (Florida State Archives.)

Capt. John Jackson Dickison of Marion County was a successful Confederate leader in the Civil War. He and his troops captured outposts along the St. Johns River and sank the Union naval vessel, *Columbine*. His valiant efforts kept federal troops from occupying Marion and Alachua Counties during the war. (Florida State Archives.)

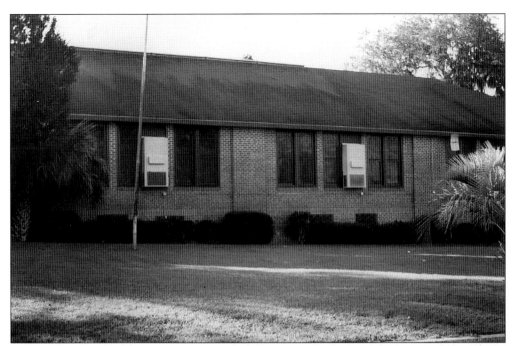

Pictured here in their current building, the Freedmen's Bureau, with financing from Northern benefactors, organized Howard Academy, a school for African Americans, in Ocala in 1867. An early building of the school between Sixth and Seventh Streets on the east side of Ocala burned around 1887 and was replaced in 1888 by a facility in west Ocala on Academy Street (Northwest Seventh Avenue) between Adams (Second Street) and Jefferson (Third Street). (Florida State Archives.)

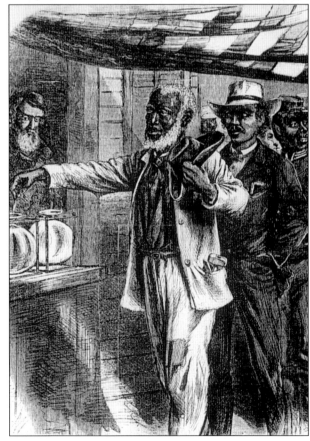

When former male slaves were given the right to vote for the first time, they took their responsibility seriously, as seen here. During the era of Reconstruction after the Civil War, both races struggled to adapt to the new situation. (Florida State Archives.)

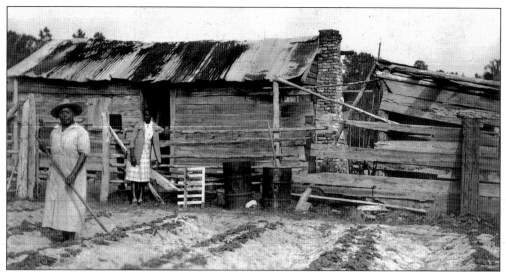

Conditions for freed slaves did not improve very much, and many of them had to live in shacks, like the one above. Today, Howard Academy houses Marion County's Black History Museum, which inducts members into its Black Archives Hall of Fame. (Florida State Archives.)

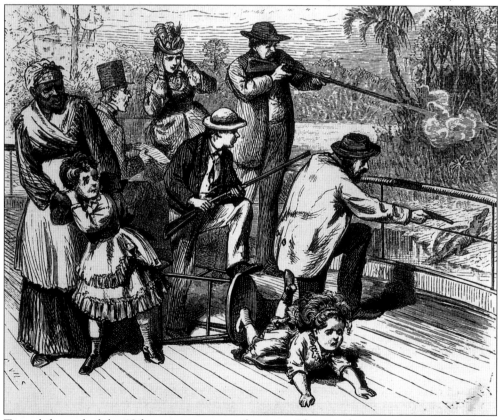

Toward the end of the 19th century, more and more residents and tourists came to the Ocala area. Shooting alligators from the safety of a steamer on the Ocklawaha River was a favorite sport for wealthy visitors. (Florida State Archives.)

Ocala's Robert Anderson, who was admitted to the bar in 1883, was president of the Florida State Bar Association in 1907. He was one of several prominent Ocalans who did well on the state level in politics; others are Wallace Sturgis Sr. (president of the Florida Senate), Farris Bryant (governor), William Chappell Jr. (Speaker of the Florida House of Representatives), Jim Williams (state senator, lieutenant governor), and Buddy MacKay (member of the U.S. House of Representatives, lieutenant governor, and governor). (Florida State Archives.)

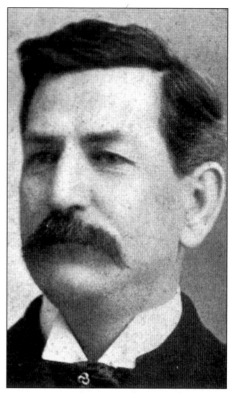

This 1883 view of buildings on the west side of Courthouse Square in Ocala shows the early home of the *Ocala Banner*, one of the town's early newspapers. In fact, a dozen newspapers, including two published by African Americans, appeared in the 1880s, although many of them merged or went out of business. Before the end of World War II, the *Ocala Morning Banner* and *Ocala Evening Star* were bought by a chain of newspapers and merged to become the *Ocala Star-Banner*, the city's main paper today. (Florida State Archives.)

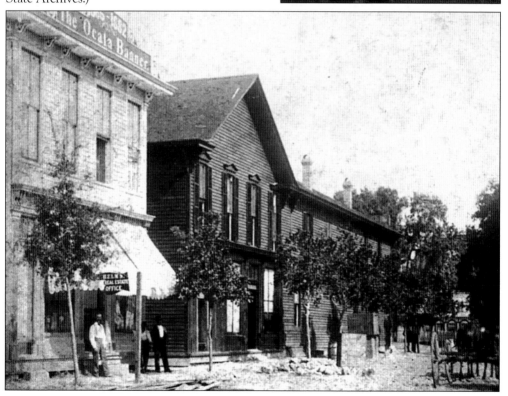

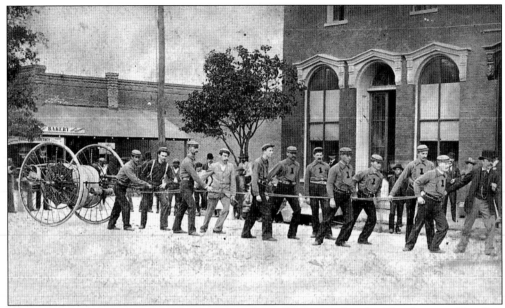

Hose Company Number 1 on Main Street was formed in 1887 after the Thanksgiving Day Fire of 1883. The speed with which the wooden structures of the town were destroyed in that and other fires convinced officials to have brick buildings constructed, especially in the downtown area, a fact that gave Ocala a new nickname: "The Brick City." (Florida State Archives.)

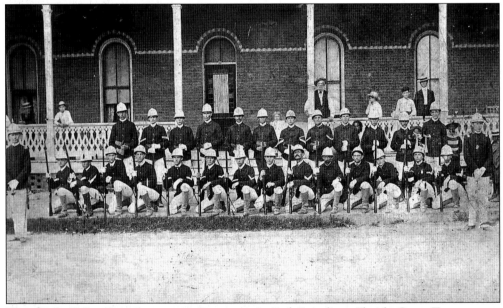

The Ocala Rifles, later known as Company A, 2nd Battalion, Florida State Troops, were organized in 1884 as a National Guard unit. The soldiers were used to keep order in Ocala and elsewhere; they built roads in Marion County and fought in Europe during World War I. The tradition of the Ocala Rifles continues in two troops stationed in Ocala today: Troop E, 153rd Cavalry and Company A, 3/20th Special Forces Group (the 351st Military Police Company). (Florida State Archives.)

An early store in downtown Ocala was Rheinauer & Brothers, which was located at Broadway and Main Streets. Dating back to 1880, when Charles Rheinauer and his brother Morritz founded a dry goods and clothing store on the west side of Courthouse Square, Rheinauers expanded in the 20th century to a group of retail clothing stores but eventually had to close. In the 1940s, Rheinauers was the oldest continuously operated business in Ocala. (Florida State Archives.)

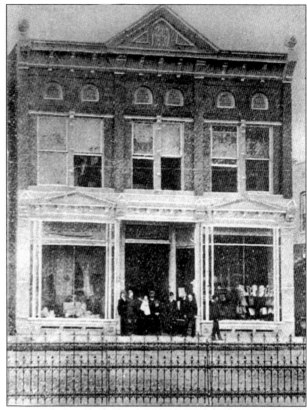

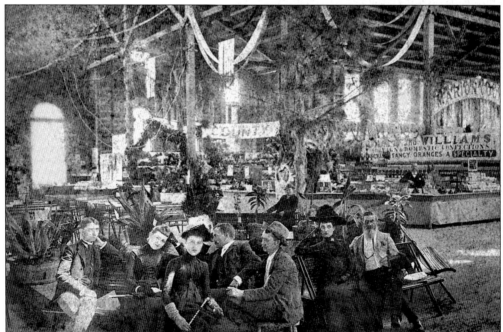

In 1889, Ocala hosted the Florida International and Semi-Tropical Exposition, pictured above, and the Populist Convention the next year. (Florida State Archives.)

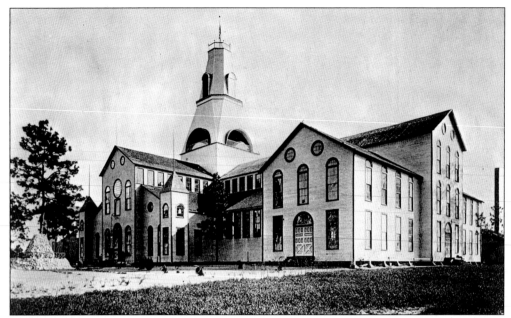

The site of the Semi-Tropical Exposition was a large, wooden building near Gerig-Webb Park on West Broadway, which was temporarily renamed Exposition Street. The large exhibit hall, topped by a tower that was visible from many miles away, had horticultural and agricultural products from Marion and other Florida counties. (Florida State Archives.)

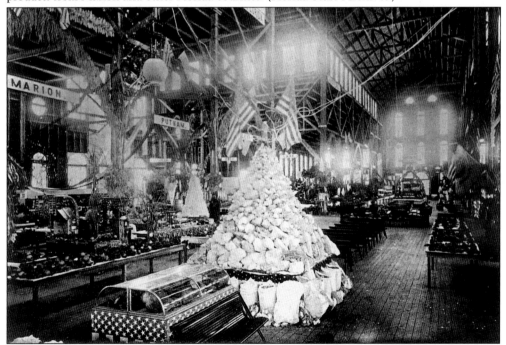

A streetcar transported many passengers from downtown Ocala to the Exposition, shown here. The Exposition, which lasted two years, demonstrated cigar making to the public and helped spawn a local tobacco industry since tobacco growing was once an important crop in Marion County. (Florida State Archives.)

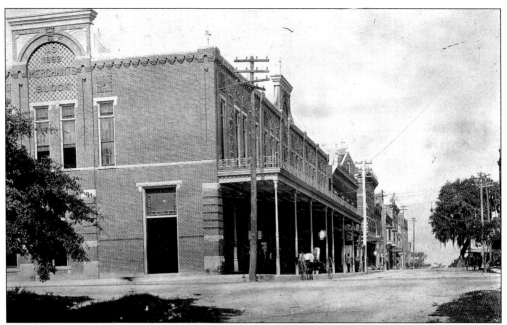

One could see horse-drawn omnibuses on Exposition Street in the late 1800s. The lack of paved streets and the presence of livestock roaming at will led to the establishment of the City Improvement Society by many of the leading women of Ocala. The formation resulted in the enforcement of city ordinances and the improvement of sanitary conditions. (Florida State Archives.)

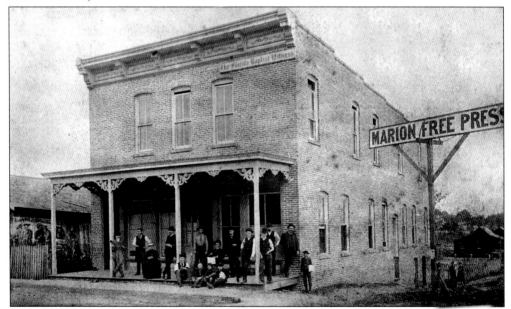

The *Marion Free Press* and *Florida Baptist Witness* were housed in the same building. The former newspaper, which began in 1886, was published by Wallace Stoval, who would later publish one of the state's most important dailies, the *Morning Tribune*. The *Florida Baptist Witness*, which had been moved from DeLand, Florida, in 1888, was a religious newspaper. (Florida State Archives.)

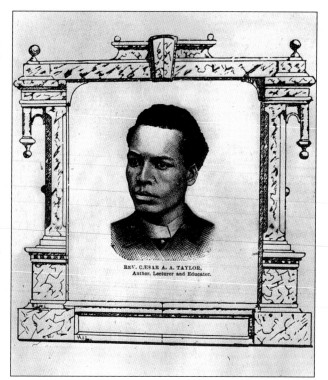

REV. CÆSAR A. A. TAYLOR,
Author, Lecturer and Educator.

One of the early African-American clergymen in Ocala was the Reverend Caesar A.A. Taylor. African Americans established their own Mount Zion African Methodist Episcopal Church soon after the Civil War. The church, located today at 623 South Magnolia Avenue, was the first brick, church building owned by African Americans in Ocala. (Florida State Archives.)

Although much of society was segregated by race in the 1800s, Ocala had several African Americans in important positions. For example, Henry W. Chandler, who was born in Maine, graduated from college, studied law at Howard University in Washington, D.C., and moved to Ocala in 1876, served as city clerk and, in 1880, was elected the state senator representing Marion County. (Florida State Archives.)

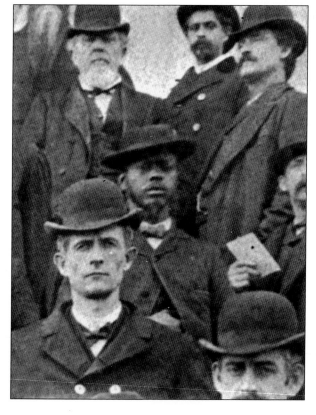

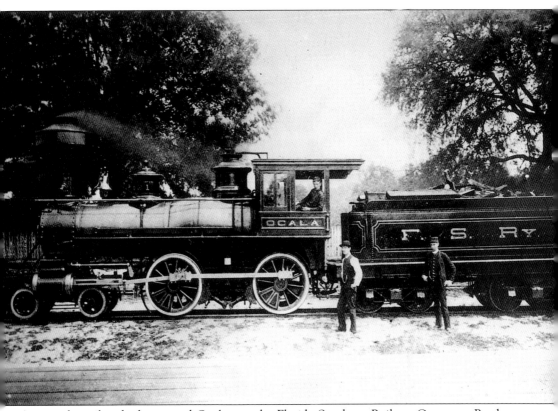

Among the railroads that served Ocala was the Florida Southern Railway Company. By the 1880s, railroads were a major means of transportation to and from the city. Some of the problems concerning railroads involved how to get freight rates comparable to other Florida cities, how to force the railroads to pay an equitable amount of property tax each year, and how to have the railroads eliminate unsightly tracks in the downtown area. (Florida State Archives.)

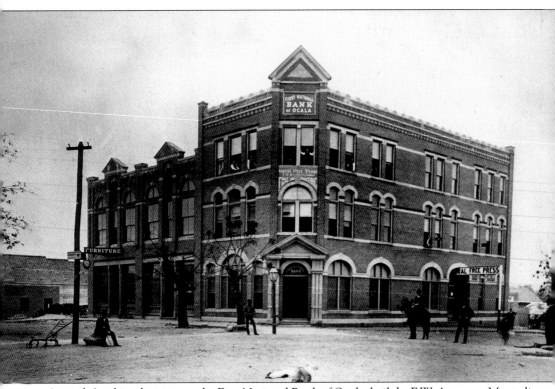

An early bank in the city was the First National Bank of Ocala, built by E.W. Agnew at Magnolia and Broadway in 1886. When the bank failed in 1895, Agnew, who had been one of the major businessmen of the city with interests in property, orange groves, and naval stores, went to federal prison for embezzlement. The First National was replaced by the Commercial Bank and Trust Company, which later became part of Sun Bank. (Florida State Archives.)

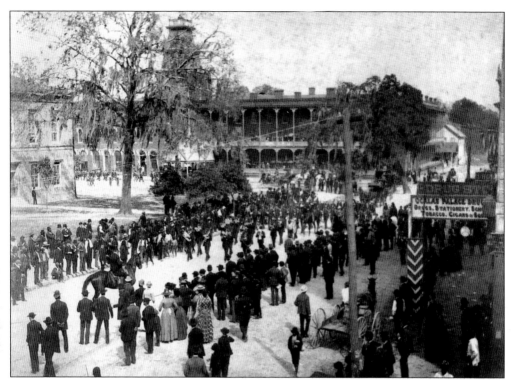

A parade at Courthouse Square on July 4, 1889, took place near the Ocala House Hotel. (Florida State Archives.)

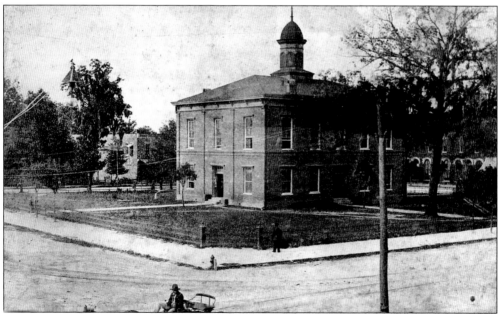

Marion County Courthouse, shown here in Ocala in 1890, served the area well for about six decades, but its inadequate design (it had no provision for offices for the circuit judge), small size, and inability to accommodate the handicapped would lead to the building of a new complex. (Florida State Archives.)

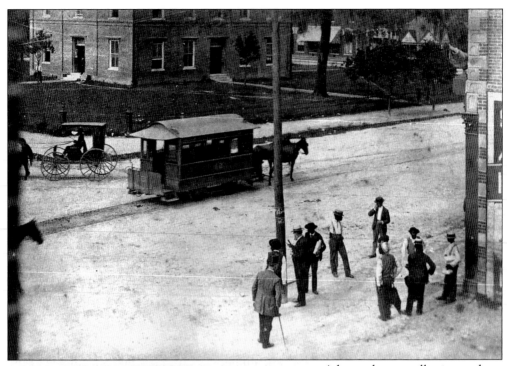

A horse-drawn trolley is seen here in front of the Marion County Courthouse in the early 1890s. (Florida State Archives.)

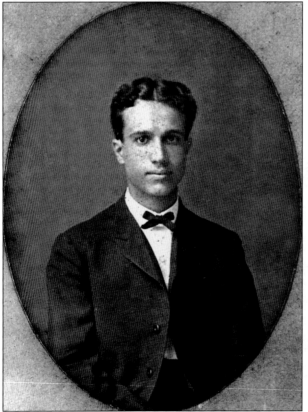

Businessman Marcus Frank came to Ocala with his mother in 1900 and assisted her in the variety store she opened. He formed a partnership with T.H. Harris in 1905 to operate the variety store. Frank was elected to the Florida House of Representatives in 1939 and 1948, and served as a city councilman for 16 years. One can still see his house at 728 Fort King Avenue in Ocala. (Florida State Archives.)

The Temple B'nai Darom was the first temple in Ocala and the third one in Florida, following synagogues in Pensacola and Jacksonville. Located at 719 Northeast Second Street, the synagogue was founded by the United Hebrews of Ocala in 1888, the same year the congregation was founded. Today, two Jewish synagogues serve the residents of Marion County. (Florida State Archives.)

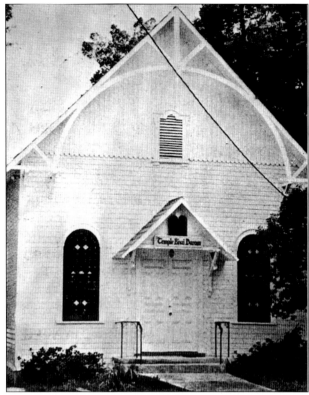

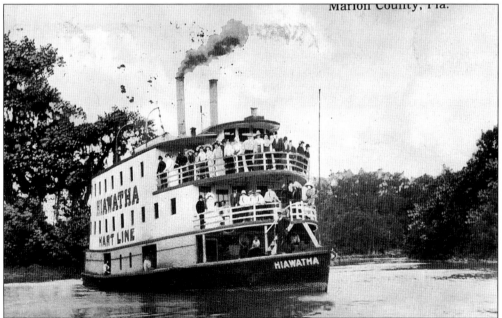

The riverboat *Hiawatha* brought visitors from Palatka to Silver Springs by way of the Ocklawaha River. The vessel's name commemorated a Native American, as did other boats on the river, such as *Osceola*, *Tuskawilla*, and *Okahumpkee*. The size of such boats was determined by the river, especially by its narrowest parts that required careful handling. (Florida State Archives.)

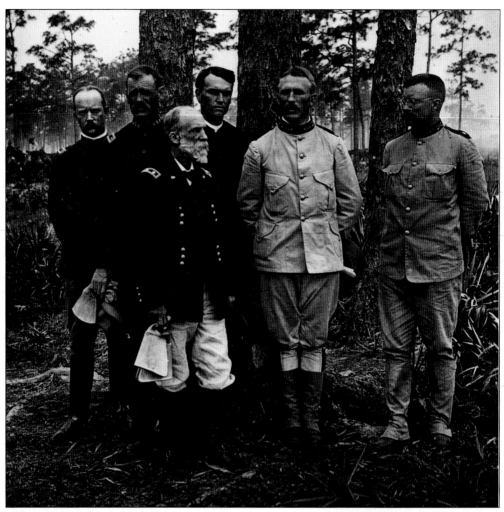

When the U.S. battleship *Maine* was sunk in Havana's harbor in 1898, the United States went to war against Spain. Among the many people who passed through Ocala on their way to Tampa and eventually Cuba to fight in that war were Col. (later President) Theodore Roosevelt and some of his "Rough Riders." While in Ocala, although he was in the midst of shaving his face, Roosevelt was persuaded to go out on the rear platform of his special train and wave to the assembled people. (Florida State Archives.)

Two

1900–1929

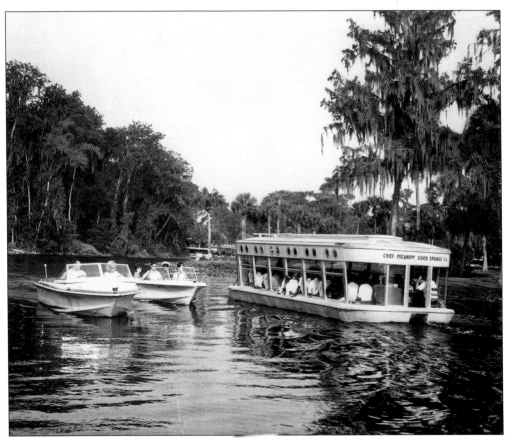

The Ocklawaha River was connected to the ill-fated Cross-Florida Barge Canal. After the Civil War and up to the 1920s, thousands of visitors made their way by boat from Jacksonville to Silver Springs by way of Palatka. The name of the river means "muddy" from the Creek language. (Florida State Archives.)

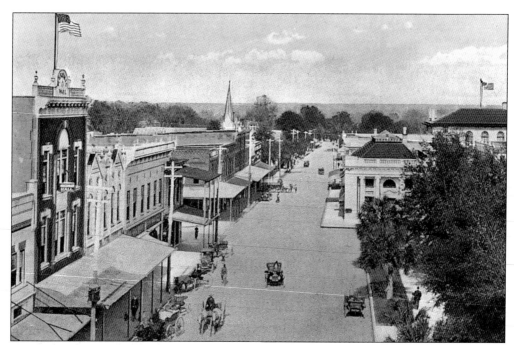

This view of downtown looking north on Magnolia Avenue shows a horse-drawn carriage. Magnolia and Main, which were the city's main north-south traffic roads, became one-way streets in 1948 in order to relieve the traffic congestion that was rapidly developing. One immediate result of the change was a reduction in the number of accidents, which had been caused by cars backing into the traffic flow from angled parking spaces. (Florida State Archives.)

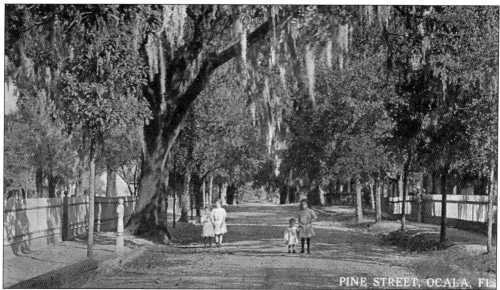

At one time, Pine Street was a tree-lined avenue where children could be seen playing. To the east of Pine was the site of an academy that was the forerunner of the University of Florida, located today in Gainesville. Pine Street later became Pine Avenue and was four-laned to be the bypass around the city's downtown area from the increasingly busy U.S. 441. (Florida State Archives.)

Mail could be collected from boxes nailed to trees along the Ocklawaha River near where the Sharps Ferry operated. Another unusual way for the mail to be collected around Ocala was by pole. The postmaster would hang outgoing mail on a pole near the railroad tracks. When the train would come through, especially in the small towns where the train would not stop, men on the train would throw off incoming mail and hook the outgoing mail from the pole. (Florida State Archives.)

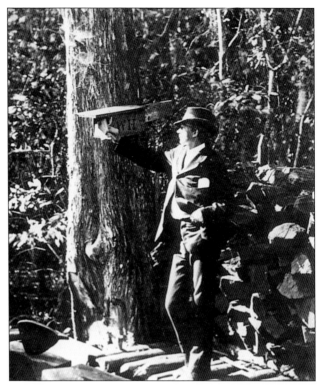

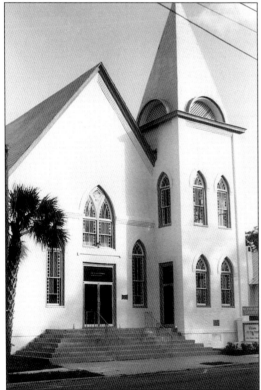

Mount Zion African Methodist Episcopal Church at 623 South Magnolia Avenue was established by freed slaves in 1866, right after the Civil War. The brick building, which is on the National Register of Historic Places, replaced the original wood-frame structure in 1881. The so-called "big brick church" has been an important part of downtown Ocala for more than 100 years. (Kevin M. McCarthy.)

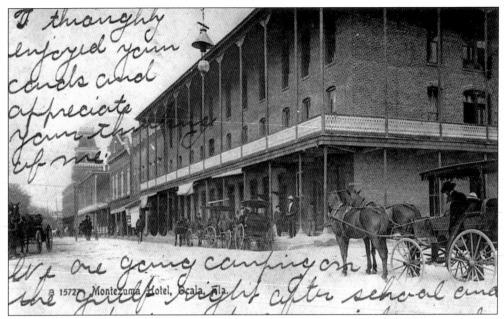

An early downtown hotel was the Montezuma, which was later renamed the Harrington Hall Hotel after one of the sons of the new owner. It became an important part of Ocala at Main and Fort King because it had housed for a time the Greyhound bus line's station. The Montezuma, built soon after the disastrous 1883 fire, used brick instead of the flammable wood that had been used in most buildings before then. (Florida State Archives.)

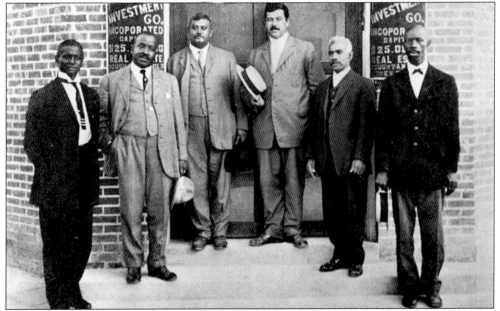

Black businessmen in the early 1900s helped establish Ocala's Metropolitan Savings Bank on South Magnolia. One of the early founders of that bank was James LaRoche, a leader in the black community and a steward at Mount Zion AME Church for over 40 years. After the bank closed in 1928 because of the Florida real estate bust, the building was converted into the Eagle Furniture Store. (Florida State Archives.)

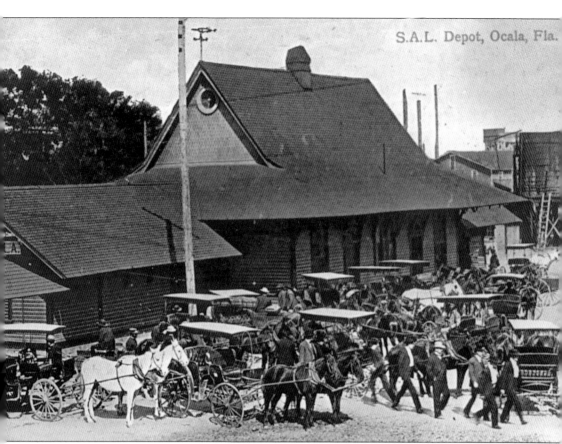

This scene from the early 1900s shows the Seaboard Air Line Depot, which was located one block west of the present Union Station near the northwest corner of North Magnolia and Van Buren Street (now Northwest Sixth Street). The horse-drawn carriages transported passengers to and from the hotels downtown. (Florida State Archives.)

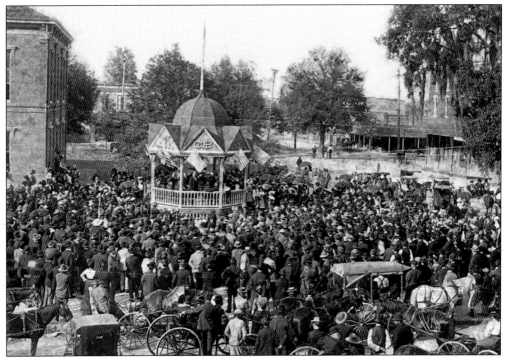

William Jennings Bryan, the Democratic Presidential nominee in 1896, visited Ocala numerous times and made speeches on at least three occasions. Here he is shown speaking to a large crowd from the Gazebo in the city's Courthouse Square. (Florida State Archives.)

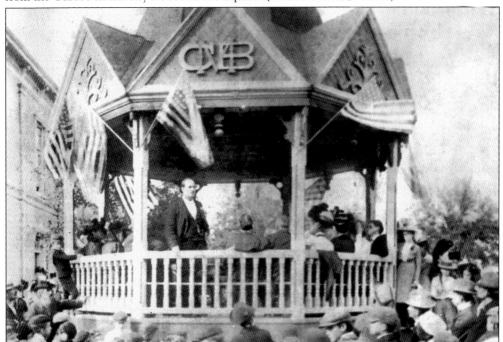

A close-up of Bryan, when he spoke in Ocala in 1908, shows the "silver-tongued orator" in the Gazebo. (Florida State Archives.)

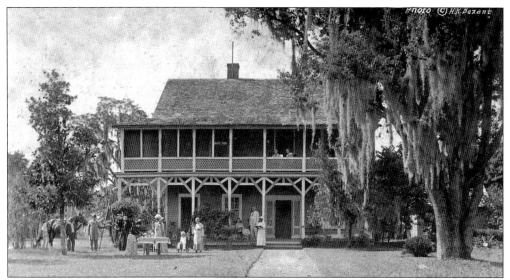

This is the home of Brig. Gen. Robert Bullock, a Confederate officer in the Civil War who later served as judge of probate and was elected to the House of Representatives in 1888 and 1890. John Breckinridge, secretary of war for the Confederacy during the Civil War and a former vice president of the United States, spent a night in Bullock's home on his escape south from Union forces in 1865. (Florida State Archives.)

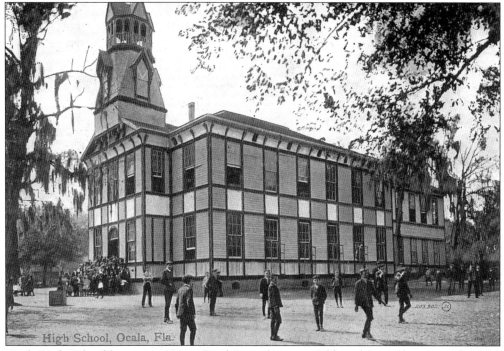

Ocala High School began in 1890 on Pond Street between Fifth and Sixth Streets on the same site where the East Florida Seminary had been. That first high school held 11 grades meeting in one building. A new high school (now Eighth Street Elementary) was built in 1914 on Southeast Eighth Street, and another new high school (now Osceola Middle) followed in 1924 at Alvarez and Fourth Streets. (Florida State Archives.)

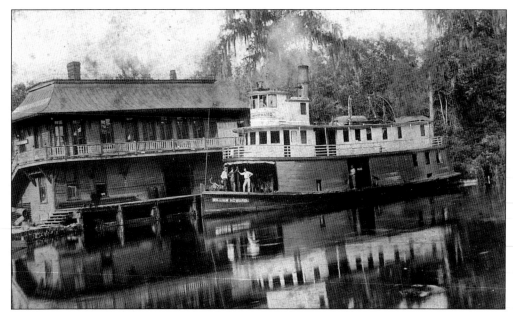

The *William Howard* steamer at Silver Springs brought passengers from cities to the east and northeast such as Palatka and Jacksonville. These steamers were able to navigate the Ocklawaha's narrow channel, swift current, and sharp turns. (Florida State Archives.)

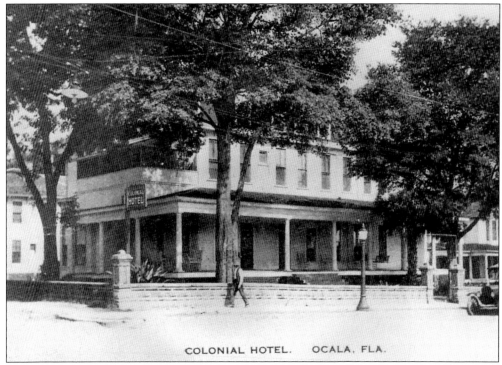

COLONIAL HOTEL. OCALA, FLA.

The Colonial Hotel began life in the early 1890s as Central Hotel on the northwest corner of Magnolia and West Adams (Northwest Second Street). It then became the St. Dennis around 1900, the Glenwood Hotel around 1906, followed by the Metropole Hotel two years later, and finally the Colonial around 1912. (Florida State Archives.)

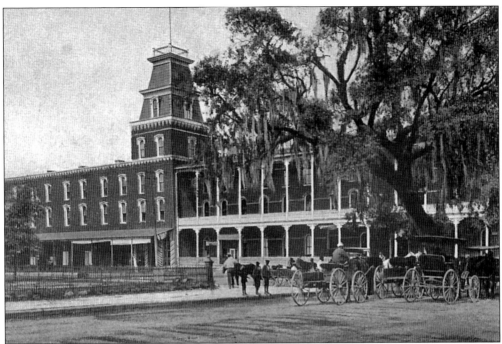

The Ocala House Hotel was on the east side of Main Street between Broadway and Ocklawaha, a site now occupied by the Ocala/Marion County Chamber of Commerce. The original hotel, which was built in 1848, destroyed in 1883, and rebuilt in 1884, became part of Henry Plant's railroad-hotel system that stretched down to Tampa and brought many tourists to Ocala. (Florida State Archives.)

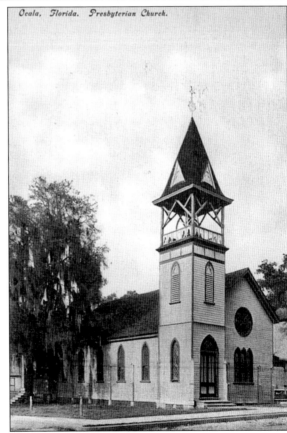

Ocala, Florida. Presbyterian Church.

The First Presbyterian Church of Ocala was dedicated in 1887 at the intersection of Fort King and Watula, later moving to Southeast Third Street in 1927. The church had the city's largest bell, and its deep sound sometimes resembled that of a fire bell. In 1946, the Reverend John McMurray, who had served as pastor of the church for 17 years, returned to Ocala for the burning of the mortgage of the church, signifying its freedom from debt. (Florida State Archives.)

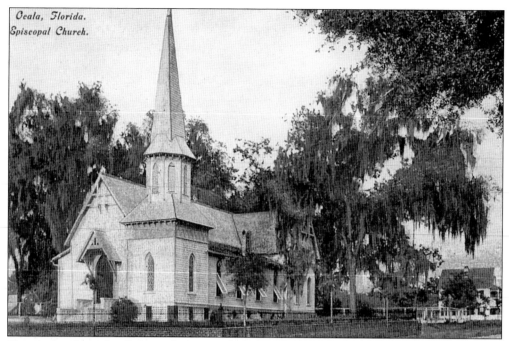

Documents show that Episcopalians were living in the area as far back as 1849, but they had to rely on visiting missionaries for services. Grace Episcopal Church parish began in 1853, and their church building was constructed in 1880 at Washington and Orange Streets. This photo shows Grace Church at its later location, built in 1906, at Watula and East Broadway. (Florida State Archives.)

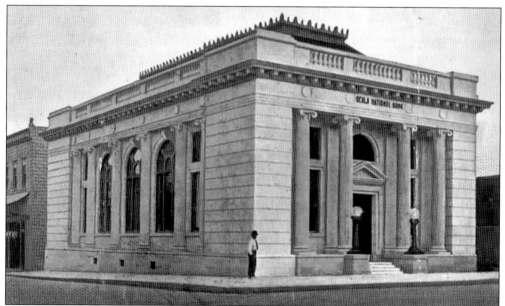

The Ocala National Bank, shown here around 1914, was housed in a neo-classical bank building constructed in 1910–1911 of Indiana limestone on the northeast corner of Ocklawaha Avenue (later renamed Silver Springs Boulevard) and Magnolia Avenue. In 1936, it became part of the Florida National Bank group controlled by Alfred DuPont. (Florida State Archives.)

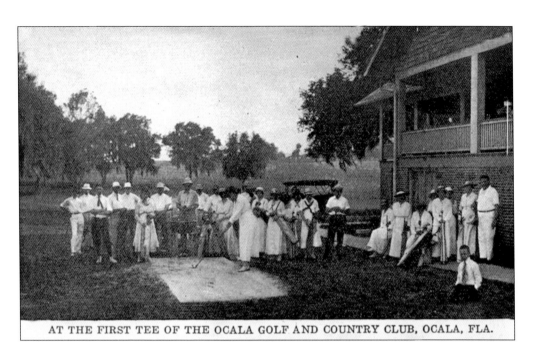

AT THE FIRST TEE OF THE OCALA GOLF AND COUNTRY CLUB, OCALA, FLA.

The Ocala Golf and Country Club was developed around 1911 as a private, nine-hole golf course. The owner was Clarence Camp, who had been state amateur golf champion and later served for many years as president of the Florida State Golf Association. The club would operate the city's only golf course until Highlands Golf Course was opened in the early 1930s. (Florida State Archives.)

William Gober practiced law (1910–1918) in Ocala at the beginning of his career and served as a judge (1917) there before becoming the U.S. attorney for the Southern District of Florida (1921–1929). (Florida State Archives.)

43

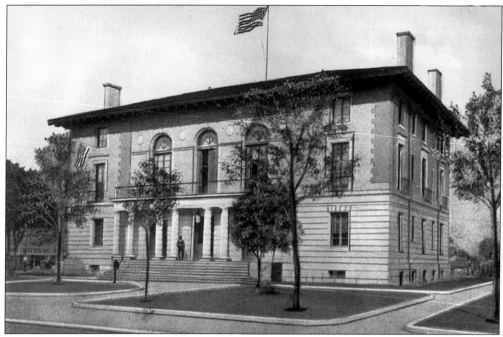

The Ocala Post Office, which opened in 1909 on Washington Street (Northeast First Street) near the Hotel Marion, was built at a time when the population of Ocala was under 5,000. When the front wall of the building eventually began to sink, causing a hazard to the public, workers had to construct a fence across the front of the building in the 1940s to prevent the public from entering that way. (Florida State Archives.)

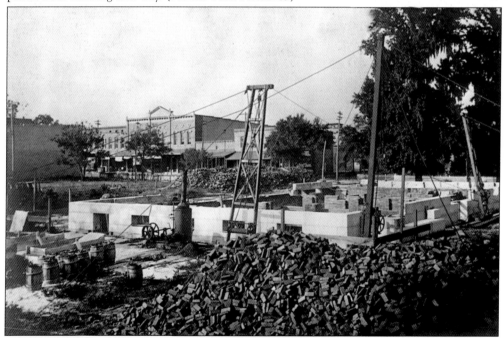

This photograph shows the construction of the federal courthouse and post office building in 1908. (Florida State Archives.)

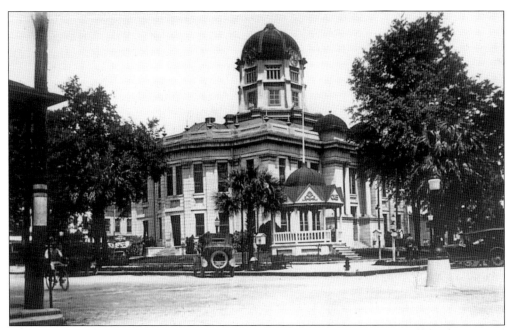

The courthouse was a beautiful building, but it would soon prove to be too small for the growing city and county it served. (Florida State Archives.)

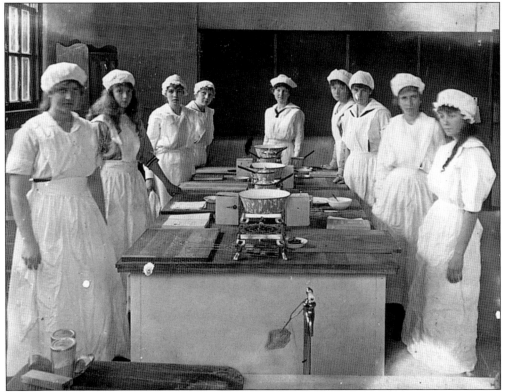

A cooking class in Ocala advertised its "Toothsome tasty wholesome cooking." (Florida State Archives.)

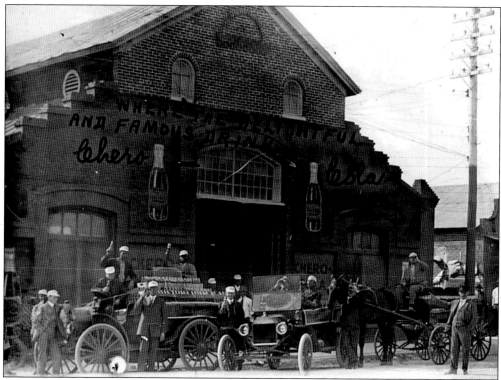

Employees of the Chero Cola Bottling Company were photographed outside their plant in the late 1910s. (Florida State Archives.)

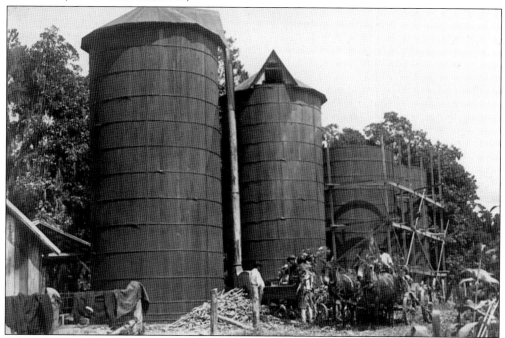

The area around Ocala continued to produce abundant agricultural products, as represented in this 1916 photo of the Edwards Brothers farm. (Florida State Archives.)

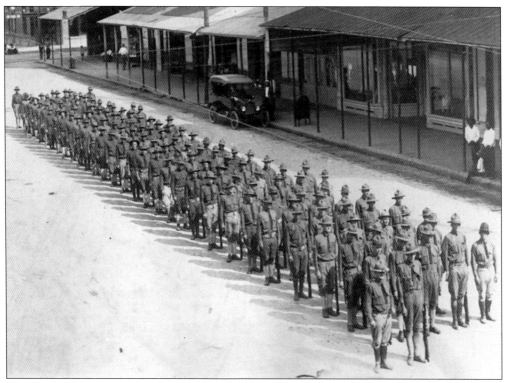

The Ocala Volunteers were photographed in 1918. (Florida State Archives.)

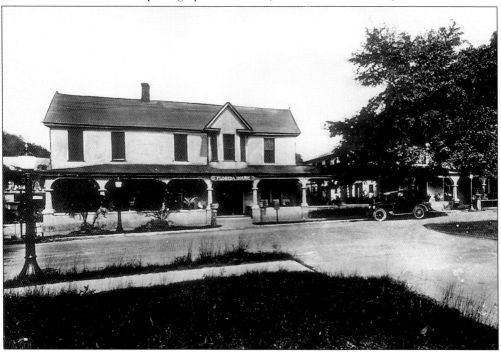

The Florida House Hotel used to be on the east side of North Magnolia across from the old bus station in the 1920s but was razed in the 1970s. (Florida State Archives.)

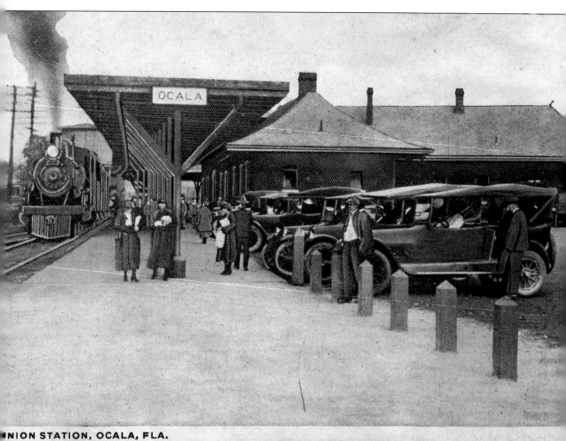

NION STATION, OCALA, FLA.

The local Union Station in the 1920s was a popular gathering place, especially its Railroad Restaurant. W.H. "Shorty" Davidson, who later joined with Carl Ray to develop Silver Springs into a very important and popular tourist attraction, ran the restaurant. (Florida State Archives.)

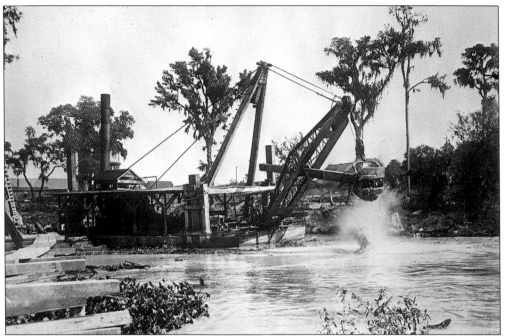

Phosphate, which is still used in fertilizers, brought much wealth to the area after it was discovered in 1889 near today's Dunnellon. The phosphate boom continued until World War I closed off the European markets. Today, Marion County still has rich deposits of phosphate, but the expense and difficulty of mining, crushing, and washing it have kept it in the ground. (Florida State Archives.)

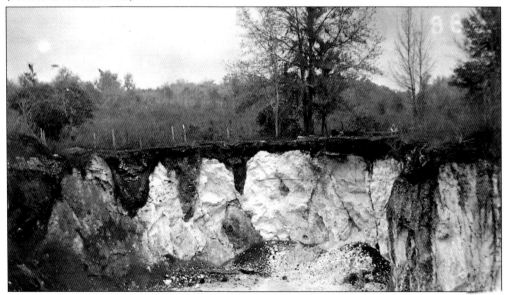

The area around Ocala was also rich in limestone, an important building material in the construction of hard-surface roads. As shown in this photograph, the limestone was often quite close to the surface and easily extracted. Limerock was mined at 11 mines around the county and produced much wealth. Ocala's Dixie Lime and Stone Company consolidated many of the mines in the 1960s. (Florida State Archives.)

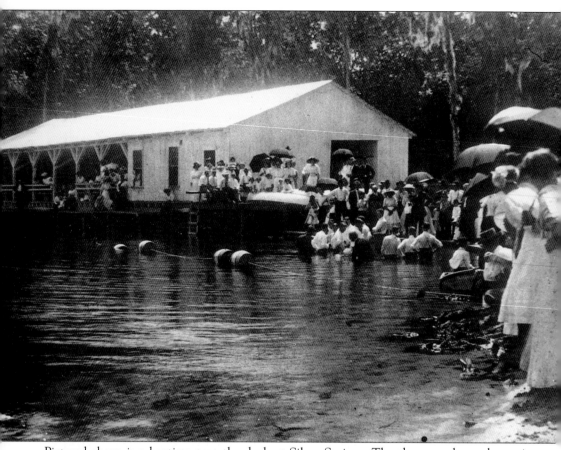

Pictured above is a baptism near the dock at Silver Springs. The theme park was becoming one of the top tourist destinations in Florida, along with Cypress Gardens in Winter Haven and Marineland below St. Augustine. The popularity of the Springs, even during the Great Depression of the 1930s, brought in much needed income since travelers usually went by car, which helped service stations and nearby hotels and motor courts. (Florida State Archives.)

Three

1930s

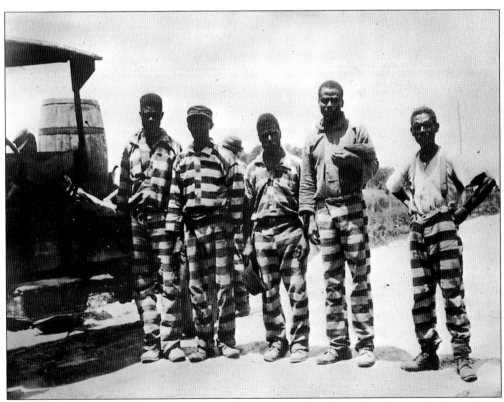

Road building became an important part of opening up Florida to the thousands of people on the move in the 1920s and 1930s. Like other counties, Marion County used convicts to build and maintain its roads, as shown in this photograph from 1928. Eventually the county established a prison complex and farm called Maricamp in southeast Ocala. (Florida State Archives.)

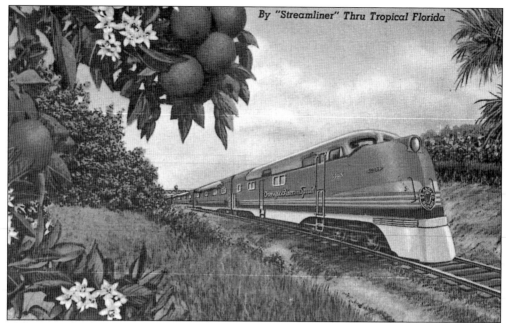

Florida's growing railroad system in the 1920s and 1930s also brought many people to the state. Beginning in the winter of 1924–1925, the Seaboard Air Line's Orange Blossom Special began its New York-to-Miami run, passing through Ocala with its luxurious train. That train, and others such as the *Silver Meteor*, the *Southern States Special*, and the *New York Florida Limited*, would have air conditioning, observation cars, and club lounges. (Florida State Archives.)

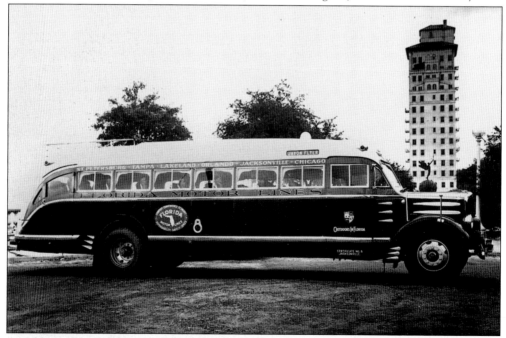

Another mode of transportation popular at the time was the bus. One of the bus lines serving Ocala was the Florida Motor Lines, which connected the city to Orlando and places along the east coast of the state. (Florida State Archives.)

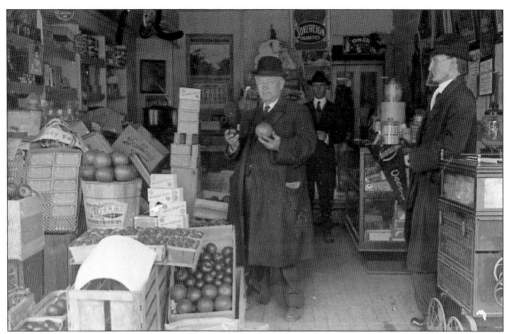

Sid Whaley, shown above at the right, ran Whaley's Grocery Store, which was south of Courthouse Square. He was known for always wearing a hat and overcoat. (Florida State Archives.)

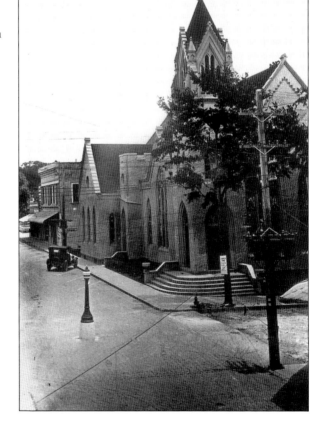

The Methodist Episcopal Church, shown here in the 1920s, had the first church built in Ocala. The site, dating back to 1850, was at the southeast corner of Fort King and South Main Street. The building, which was partly constructed by slaves, had a gallery for slaves who were members of the congregation. (Florida State Archives.)

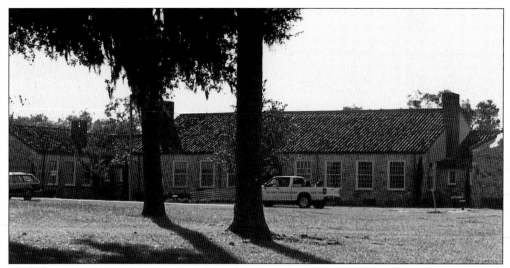

The Fessenden Elementary School, which was established in 1868 (three years after the end of the Civil War), provided educational opportunities for many African Americans over 12 decades. Fessenden Elementary is a public school, as opposed to the private Fessenden Academy, which was established in 1898 to honor Ferdinand Stone Fessenden, a wealthy businessman from Boston who helped pay for the school. The facility at 4200 Northwest Ninetieth Street is an integrated elementary school. (Kevin M. McCarthy.)

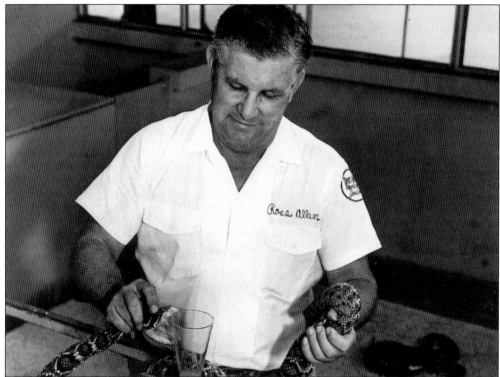

Ross Allen, seen here at the Silver Springs Serpentarium, opened a taxidermist shop there in 1929 and later a facility where he could milk rattlesnakes for the venom that could save the lives of those bitten by snakes. (Florida State Archives.)

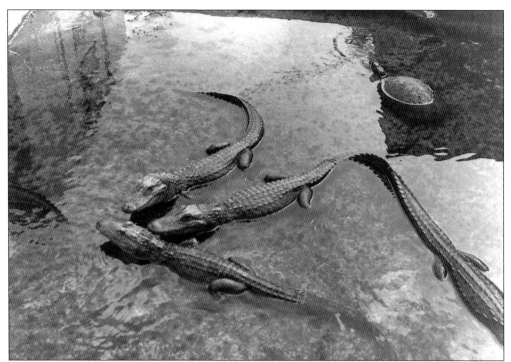

Ross Allen's Reptile Institute had live alligators on display. The Institute supplied rattlesnake serum to help in the fight against arthritis, rheumatic pains, and neuralgia. One can still see alligators and alligator wrestling at the popular Silver Springs. (Florida State Archives.)

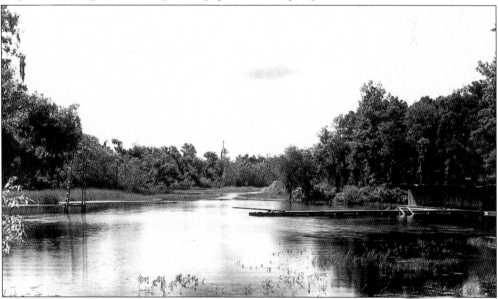

Nearby Blue Springs, which was between Ocala and Dunnellon, was one of the many attractions in the area. Frank Greene, an attorney from New York who had moved to Ocala, chose the name in 1934 as he developed a resort featuring boats that allowed visitors to look beneath the water. It would later become Rainbow Springs in the 1930s when it tried to compete with the very popular Silver Springs. (Florida State Archives.)

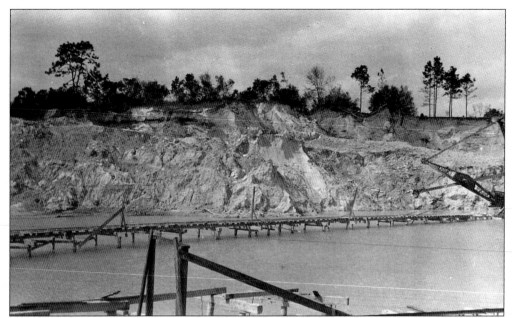

Phosphate, which had provided a good income to the people in and around Ocala, as well as some 20 mining companies, was much less important to the local economy when World War I closed off European markets and more easily mined phosphate was discovered elsewhere. (Florida State Archives.)

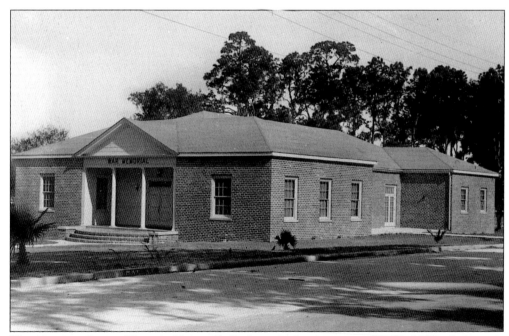

The American Legion Home in Tuscawilla Park was built as a memorial to World War I veterans. The War Memorial Swimming Pool on Anthony Road (presently Northeast Eighth Avenue) was another fitting way to remember local soldiers who had served in American wars. The person chosen to direct the pool was local star swimmer, Newt Perry. (Florida State Archives.)

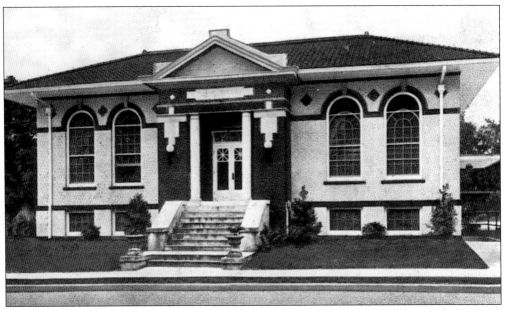

Ocala's public library, which opened in 1916, was started by a number of Ocalans, including Miss Lou Gamsby, who convinced the Carnegie Foundation to build it. She served as librarian there from 1916 until 1951, at which time Jewel Garvin of Atlanta replaced her. "Miss Lou" had guided the reading habits of many residents of Ocala and would not allow the local children to read books that she judged were unsuitable. The local library became the Central Florida Regional Library in 1961 and served Marion, Citrus, and Levy Counties. (Florida State Archives.)

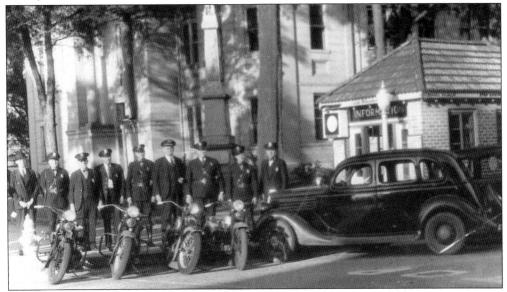

The Ocala Police Department posed for this photo in 1935. From left to right are Charley Hamer "Duffy" Marlowe, Walter Elliott, P.F. Chester, Irvin Devaney, A.L. Connell, Chief John Spencer, Roger Lyles, Harry Bostick, and C.C. Tyler. Spencer, who had been appointed police chief in 1934, had a long history in Ocala, including working as a locomotive engineer, establishing the Ocala Gas Engine Works, operating the first Buick automobile agency in Florida, and then serving as police chief for 18 years. (Florida State Archives.)

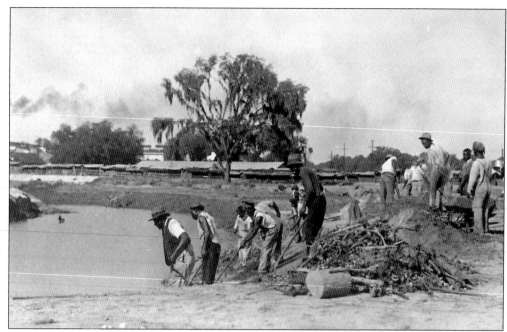

Workers built the Tuscawilla Park tennis courts in 1935. A public swimming pool at the park was dedicated by the War Memorial Association to all those from Marion County who served their country in war. The park was named in honor of a Native American maiden of that name who supposedly died in a grotto in what became the city park. (Florida State Archives.)

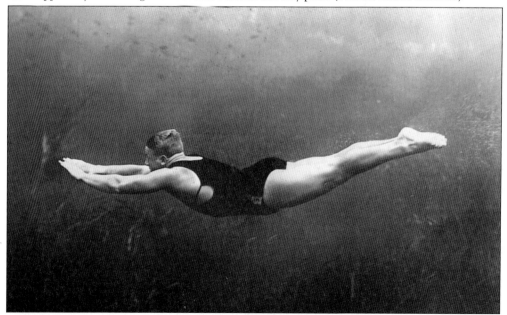

Newt Perry, whom writer Grantland Rice called the best swimmer of the time, trained many of this country's swimming stars, founded the water ballet team at Weeki Wachee Springs, trained actors and actresses for swimming scenes, and appeared in many of the movies filmed at Silver Springs in the 1930s and 1940s. In 1941, he set the world record for deep diving without equipment: 187 feet. (Florida State Archives.)

President Franklin Roosevelt launched the start of the construction of the Cross-Florida Ship Canal in 1935, an ambitious project south of Ocala that was supposed to link the Atlantic Ocean with the Gulf of Mexico. The hundreds of workers on the project brought in much income to Ocala during the Great Depression. Later changed to a barge canal, the project was killed by President Nixon in the 1970s, but actual de-authorization did not come until the 1990s. (Florida State Archives.)

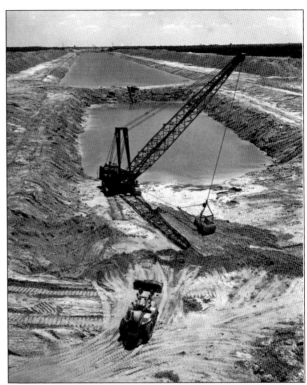

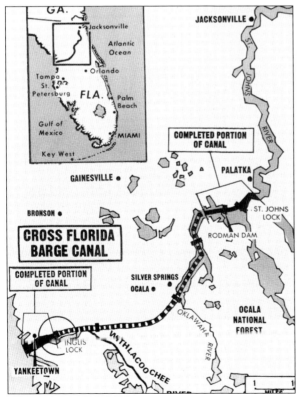

A map showing where the Florida Barge Canal would go indicates how much Ocala could expect to grow from increased trade and commerce with its access to the Atlantic Ocean and the Gulf of Mexico. (Florida State Archives.)

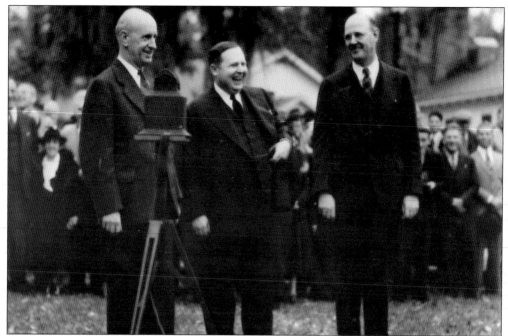

Gov. David Sholtz, center, visited Camp Roosevelt south of Ocala in 1936. The camp at the intersection of Lake Weir Avenue and U.S. 441 was the administrative center for the construction crews working on the canal. The camp later became the residential Roosevelt Village, and the planned canal became the Cross Florida Greenway State Recreation Area, with 40,000 acres in Marion County. (Florida State Archives.)

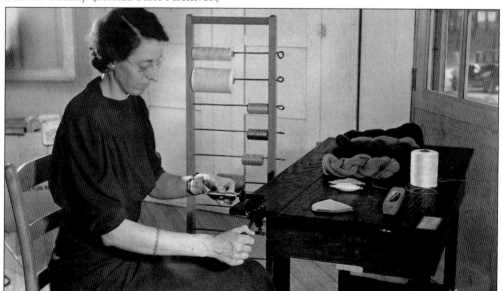

Camp Roosevelt was the site of a vocational school that taught many skills to its students, including weaving. The co-educational school, operated in the 1940s by the National Youth Administration (NYA), the U.S. Department of Education, and the Marion County School Board, taught skills to hundreds of students—skills that were especially useful for the war effort. (Florida State Archives.)

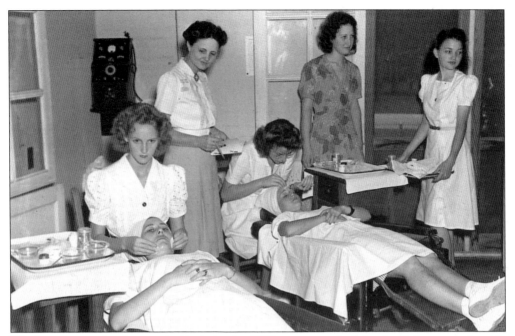

The beautician school set up in Ocala by the NYA was part of a federal relief program for girls who had dropped out of other schools. Eleanor Roosevelt, the wife of the President, organized the NYA because she felt that the Depression relief programs were geared for men. In this school, the girls attended classes for half a day, then worked the rest of the day on special projects like sewing clothing. (Florida State Archives.)

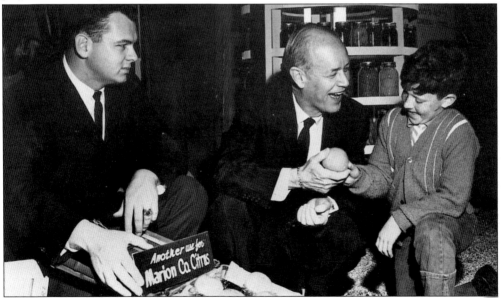

For decades farmers had tried, with varying degrees of success, to grow citrus trees in and around Ocala, but the occasional freezes that hit North Florida drove most of those farmers into other fields. Seen here handing an orange to a boy is Ocalan Farris Bryant, who served as governor of Florida for four years (1961–1965) and helped establish the state's new universities and many two-year colleges. (Florida State Archives.)

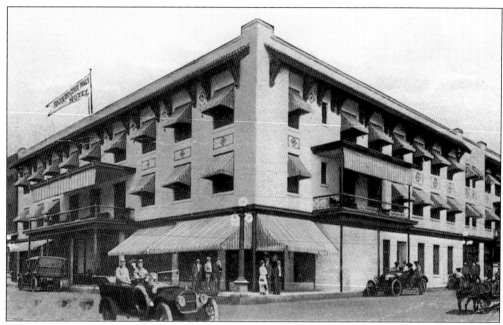

Harrington Hotel, which had been the Montezuma Hotel at one time, housed Florida Greyhound Lines in its South Main Street facility. The bus line would move out in 1946 to a new bus station on North Magnolia to help alleviate the traffic congestion caused by the large buses on South Main and Osceola. When workers remodeled the Harrington, a 75-unit hotel with 10 rental units, they added two paintings by Bob Camp, a popular, local artist. (Florida State Archives.)

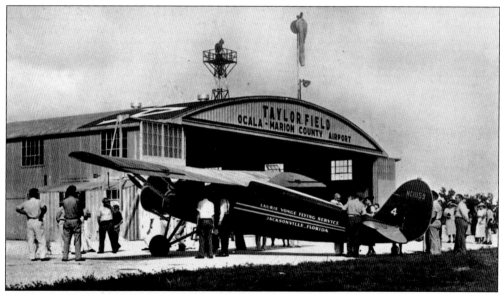

The airport that served Ocala was Taylor Field, so called because James J. Taylor and his family gave land for the airport at the southwestern edge of the city. During World War II the federal Works Progress Administration (WPA) expanded the airport's facilities to three 4,000-foot runways and two shorter ones. The size of the airport grew from the original 175 acres to 410 acres. (Florida State Archives.)

Four

1940s

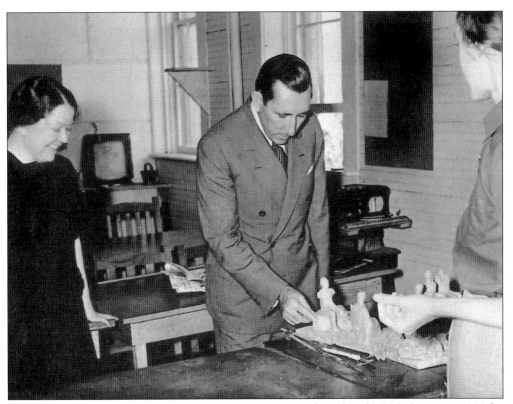

U.S. Senator Claude Pepper was a popular legislator. First elected to the U.S. Senate in 1936, he served there until 1951. Eleven years later he was elected to the U.S. House of Representatives and, in 1988, one year before he died, became the oldest person ever elected as a congressman. (Florida State Archives.)

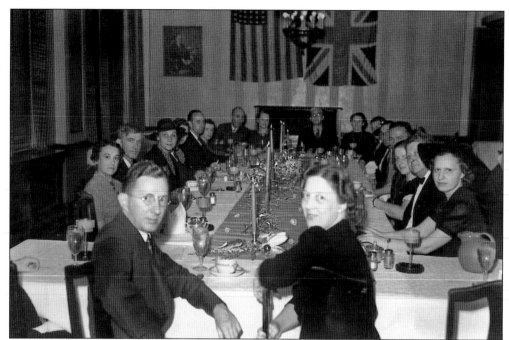

The Camp Roosevelt staff had a Christmas celebration in 1940. Although the building of the Cross-Florida Ship Canal had stopped in 1936, many were hoping it would begin again and bring jobs to the area. In 1946, the U.S. Corps of Engineers gave in to the pressure of Mayor John Marshall Green and made dozens of the empty houses at Camp Roosevelt available for rent to war veterans at low prices. (Florida State Archives.)

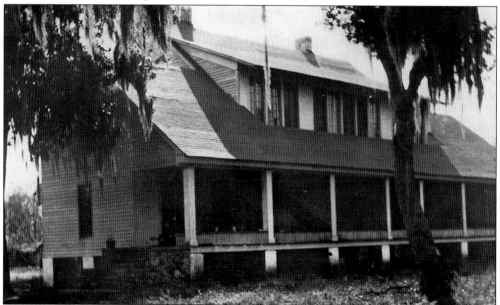

"Pine Hill" was one of the largest plantations in and around Ocala. Its workers produced their own food (other than tea and coffee), its owners taught their children at home, and the residents provided much of their own entertainment. On Sundays, the white families would often go into Ocala for church services and midday dinners with friends. (Florida State Archives.)

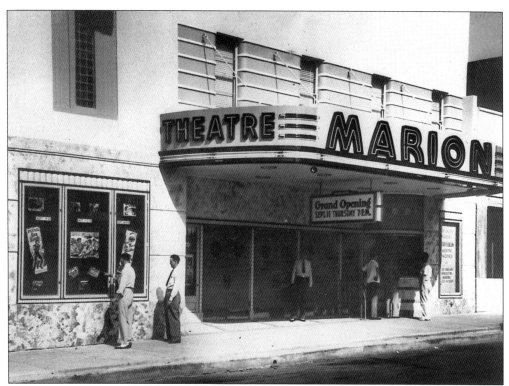

The Marion Theatre opened on South Magnolia in 1941. It joined the Dixie, the Ritz, and the Roxy. The Marion, built for about $100,000, seated almost 1,000 people and had an air conditioning system and the latest sound equipment. (Florida State Archives.)

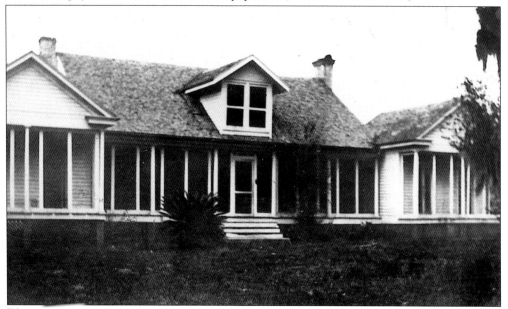

The Millwood Plantation, a 400-acre plantation built by the Owens family near Reddick, had its own sawmill, store, and other enterprises. The Waldo Plantation, which was in the southwest, at one time encompassed more than 3,000 acres of orange trees. (Florida State Archives.)

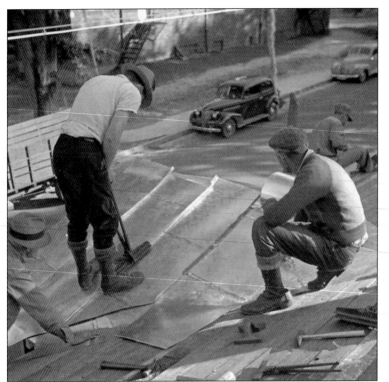

The Marion County Vocational School, shown here being built in 1941, was located at Camp Roosevelt south of Ocala in the 1940s but later moved to a building near Union Station and to the Ocala High School site. The first sessions of Central Florida Community College were held in the old vocational building adjacent to Osceola Middle School. (Florida State Archives.)

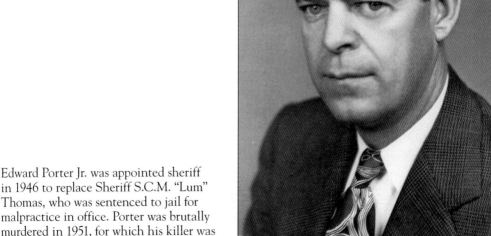

Edward Porter Jr. was appointed sheriff in 1946 to replace Sheriff S.C.M. "Lum" Thomas, who was sentenced to jail for malpractice in office. Porter was brutally murdered in 1951, for which his killer was electrocuted. (Florida State Archives.)

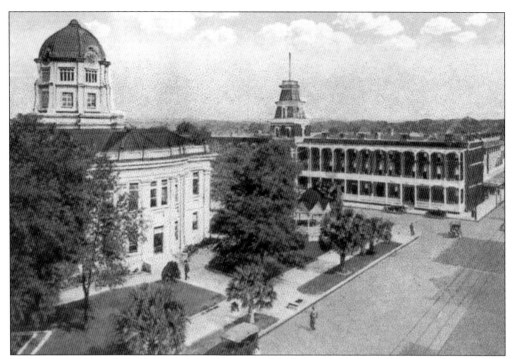

The courthouse and Ocala House are shown in the photograph above. The three-story Ocala House Hotel, which was completely remodeled in 1951, was renamed Hotel Ocala. It used to have on its ground floor the Piggly Wiggly grocery store, Swilley's Bar, and Greens Drug Store. The city of Ocala bought the hotel in the 1960s and razed it for a parking lot, but instead the site became the Chamber of Commerce building. (Florida State Archives.)

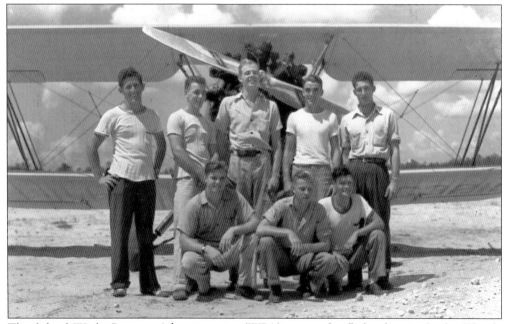

The federal Works Progress Administration (WPA) operated a flight class in Ocala. (Florida State Archives.)

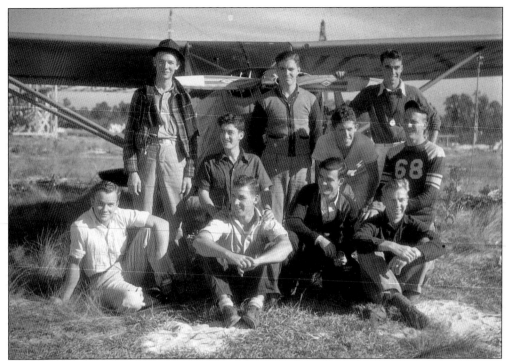

Many of the men who trained in this facility served in World War II in various aspects of aviation. (Florida State Archives.)

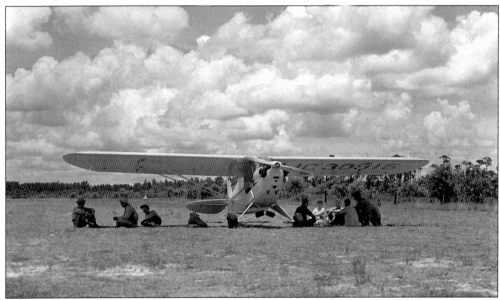

The Ocala area hosted the Greenville Aviation School during World War II as one of the aviation-training sites for the Army Air Corps established in Florida because of the good weather, flat terrain, and good flying conditions. After it closed in 1944, part of the aviation school's facilities at the Ocala Airport were used by the Brewster Shirt Corporation, which hired hundreds of women to manufacture shirts. When the plant finally closed, it became the site of the community school operated by the school board. (Florida State Archives.)

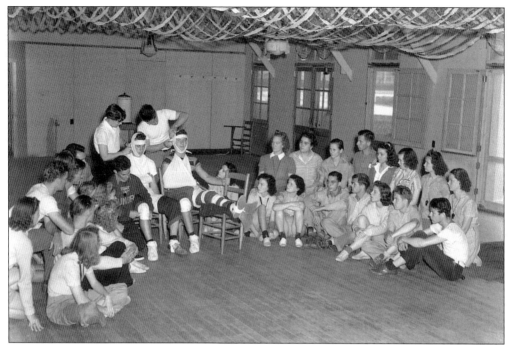

A vocational school in Ocala during World War II also offered classes in first-aid bandaging. (Florida State Archives.)

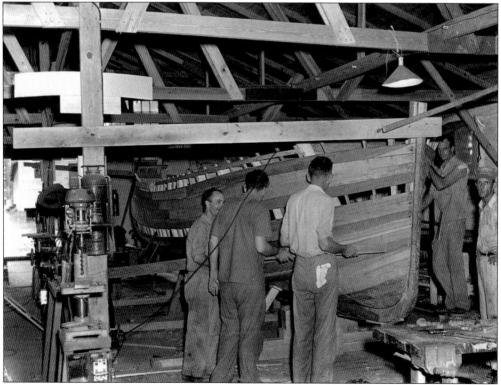

A boat-building class also proved to be a popular course. (Florida State Archives.)

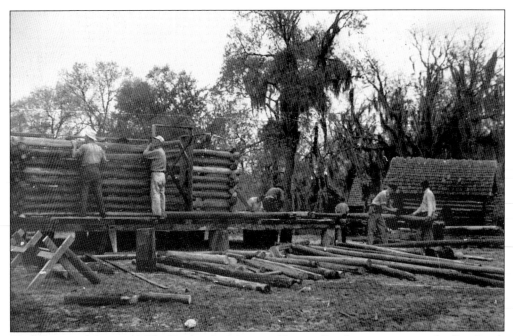

The filming of the novel *The Yearling* by Marjorie Kinnan Rawlings was set in the Big Scrub (Ocala National Forest). Pictured above is the construction of a set for the film. The author, who lived in nearby Cross Creek and won the 1939 Pulitzer Prize for her novel, was married to Norton Baskin, the manager of Ocala's Hotel Marion, built in 1926–1927 through the efforts of local citizens who wanted a facility to attract visitors. (Florida State Archives.)

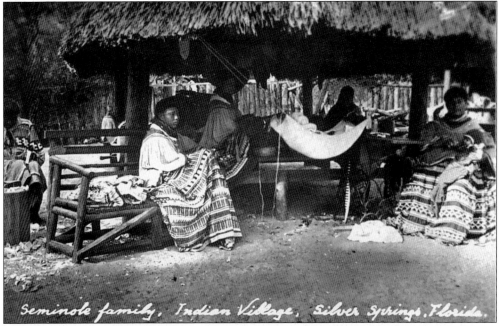

Seminole family, Indian Village, Silver Springs, Florida.

The Silver Springs park had many exhibits, including this Seminole family in an authentic Indian village in the 1940s. The Native Americans, who were brought from the Everglades, sold their colorful clothes and handmade objects to visitors. (Florida State Archives.)

A Seminole boy at Silver Springs in the 1940s is pictured here. The Seminole Village and Ross Allen's Reptile Institute appeared in short movies filmed at Silver Springs. (Florida State Archives.)

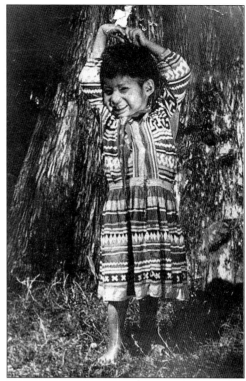

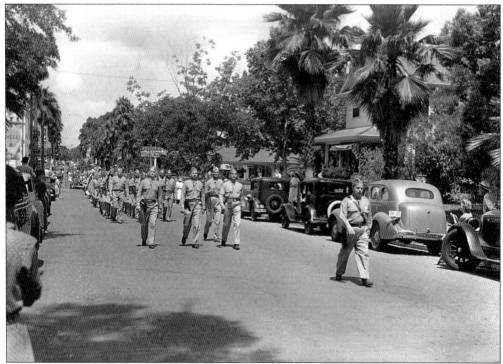

A Fourth of July parade in Ocala in 1941 brought out local residents to honor their hometown soldiers. (Florida State Archives.)

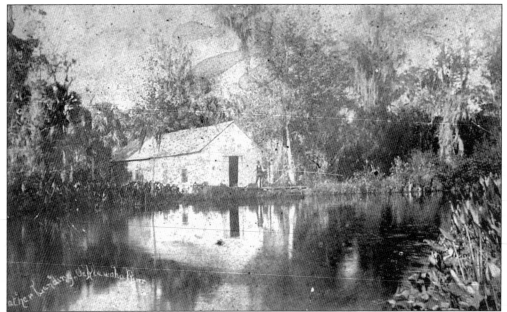

In 1945, James J. Taylor of Ocala bought nearby Heather Island, which was located on the Ocklawaha River near Candler. DeForest Hulburd, president of Elgin Watch Company, had used the private island as a winter resort. (Florida State Archives.)

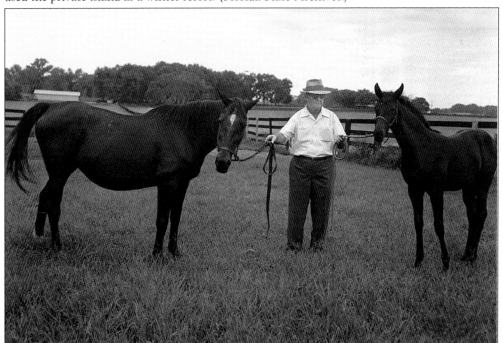

Carl G. Rose successfully raised thoroughbred horses on his Rosemere Farm on State Road 200 where Central Florida Community College later located. In 1944, when a two-year-old filly named Gornil from Rosemere Farm won a race at Miami's Tropical Park, she was the first Florida-bred horse to win a race in Florida. That would be the start of a successful string of such wins by other Florida-bred horses. (Florida State Archives.)

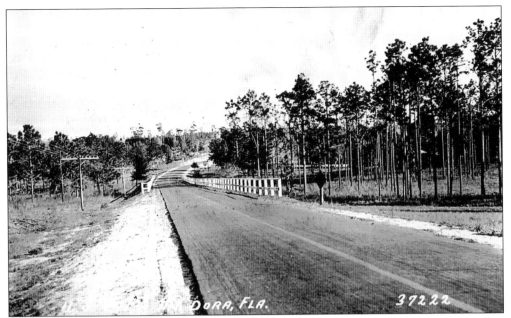

DORA, FLA.   37222

The building of U.S. 441 through Ocala brought many people to Ocala and its businesses, but its exact location caused much argument in the late 1940s and 1950s as downtown businesses worried that its location to the west of that area would hurt their businesses. In 1951, Marion Construction Company won the bid to four-lane U.S. 441 south of Ocala to Belleview. (Florida State Archives.)

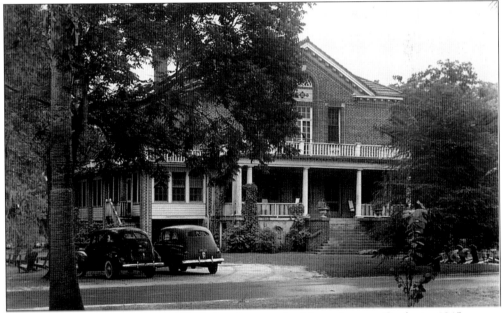

The Florida Industrial School for Girls, photographed here in east Ocala in 1945, was a correctional institution that the Florida Legislature authorized in 1915. When the state began making plans for building a similar school near Lowell, various ideas were put forth for the former facility, including that of a junior college and the headquarters for the forest fire suppression unit, but it became the county governmental complex. (Florida State Archives.)

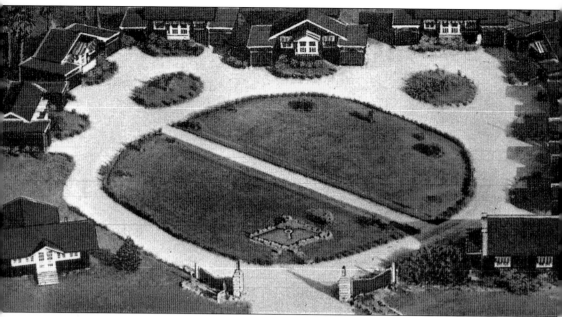

On North Magnolia, the Red Gate Colony had tourist cabins, each with its own private bath and garage, as well as heat during the winter. Its owner in the 1940s, Vivian Gahan, was one of the Ocalans who had a son killed in World War II. Harry "Shanghai" (so called because he traveled around the world twice) Gahan was killed in a bomber crash near St. Petersburg, Florida, in 1942. (Florida State Archives.)

Five

1950s

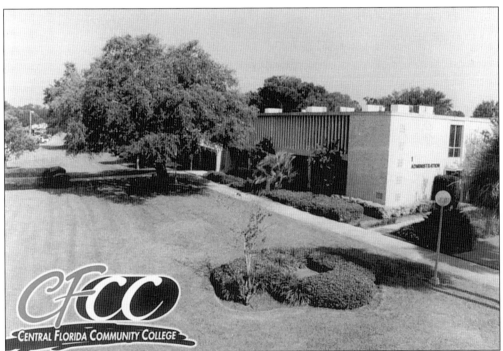

In 1958 Ocala returned to its status as a college town. The Civil War ended the East Florida Seminary (forerunner of the University of Florida) as far as Ocala was concerned, but in the 1950s a determined group of citizens worked hard for two junior colleges and won. Central Florida Junior College (the name was changed in 1971 to Central Florida Community College [CFCC]) opened its doors in 1958 under the leadership of President Kenneth Williams at the old Marion County Vocational Building located across the street from Osceola Middle School (later it was demolished). The Administration Building, seen above, was completed in late 1959 on State Road 200, and classes were held there starting in 1960. (Central Florida Community College.)

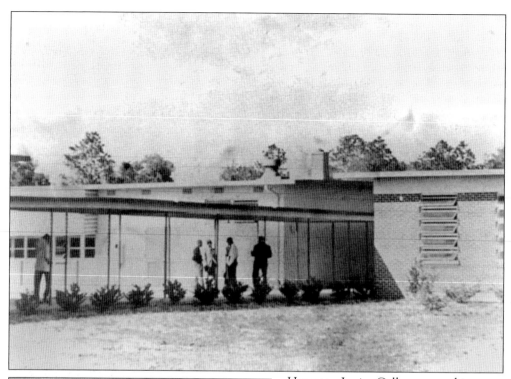

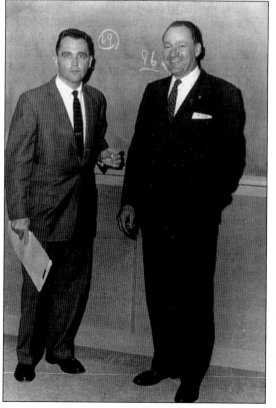

Hampton Junior College opened its doors in 1958 on West Silver Springs Boulevard under the leadership of President William H. Jackson. Hampton Junior College was one of the first black, two-year colleges in the state. Central Florida Junior College and Hampton Junior College merged on July 1, 1966, and William Jackson became a high-ranking administrator. The Hampton Center of CFCC opened in 1996 at the site of the former Florida State Fire College in West Ocala. (CFCC.)

State Representative Bill Chappell (left) was introduced by CFJC President Kenneth Williams before he spoke in 1958 to the CFJC Political Union. Later, Chappell served a number of terms as a member of the U.S. House of Representatives. (J.W. Brinson Jr.)

Ross Allen is shown in 1974 holding a record size (almost four feet long) Eastern Coral snake at the Ross Allen Reptile Institute. Naturalist Allen was a folk hero, and many brought their finds to him, with the snake being an example. The Silver Springs Attraction in pre–Interstate 75 and pre–Walt Disney World days was most popular with Americans and press, and the great herpetologist with a flair for showmanship was a stellar performer. In the movies he actually wrestled live alligators. (Ross Allen.)

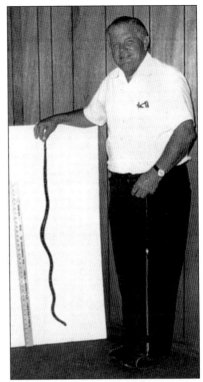

Paul Cunningham, a noted artist and sculptor, is shown applying the final stroke to one of his paintings on display at the Prince of Peace Memorial, which he created at the Silver Springs Attraction. The non-denominational chapel's emphasis stressed the life of Christ. (Silver Springs Attraction.)

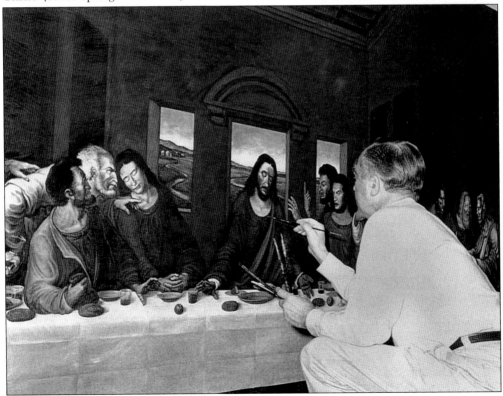

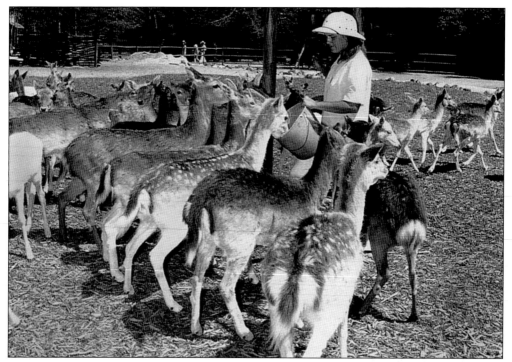

International Deer Ranch was popular with tourists who loved to pet and hand-feed deer from all over the world. The driving force was Tommy Bartlett, a national celebrity of radio and TV who hosted the popular show, *Welcome Traveler*. (Silver Springs Attraction.)

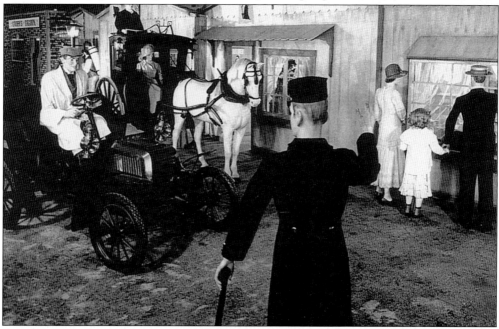

A scene from the 1890s greeted Early American Museum visitors. The museum featured one of the world's outstanding collections of antique cars and horse-drawn vehicles. (Silver Springs Attraction.)

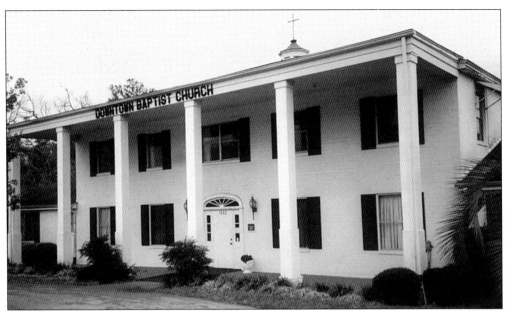

Mount Vernon Lodge, located at 1632 East Silver Springs Boulevard, was one of the most popular lodges in the 1950s in Central Florida. In 1992 Downtown Baptist Church bought the property and quickly added the cross above. (Kevin M. McCarthy.)

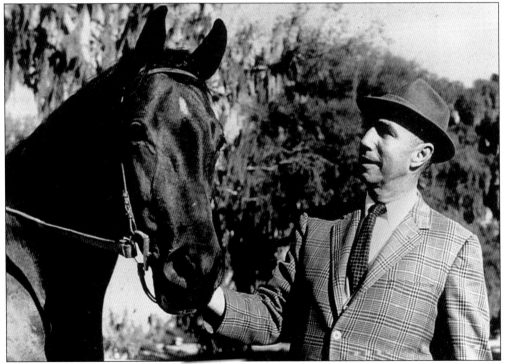

Joe O'Farrell, an owner and trainer, is shown with one of his many thoroughbreds. Knowledgeable about all facets of the horse industry, he earned just about all possible national honors. Ocala is a leading thoroughbred center of the world due to the leadership of Carl Rose, Joe O'Farrell, and a few other pioneers. (David Cook.)

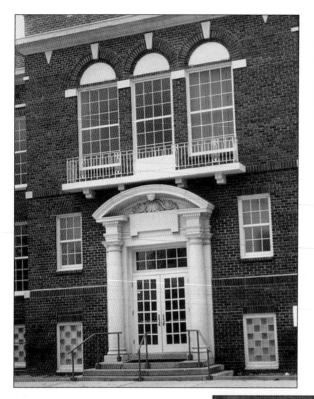

Ocala High School is seen here at the start of the 1950s; it is today called Osceola Middle School. Tom Bailey was a supervising principal of Ocala schools along his road to becoming Florida's superintendent of public instruction. (Kevin M. McCarthy.)

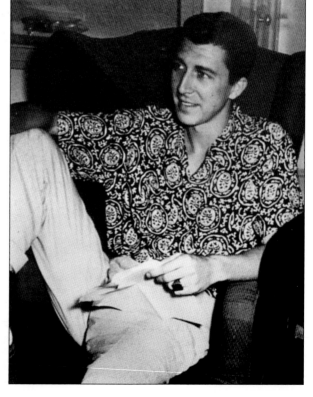

In the early 1950s, Patrick O'Neal had already earned a solid reputation as an actor who could handle many roles. Television series would follow. Like James Melton, he attended Ocala High School and the University of Florida before earning stardom in New York City. (David Cook.)

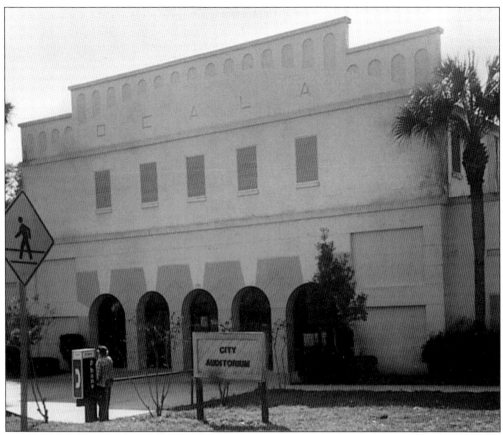

Over the decades, many musical, political, sporting, and social activities were held at City Auditorium. It is located in Tuscawilla Park. (Kevin M. McCarthy.)

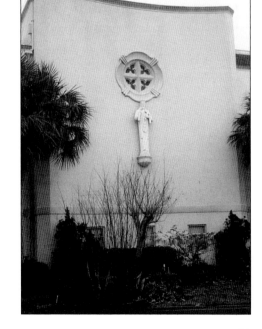

In the 1950s, Ocalans took the concern of their churches seriously, and one of the strongest churches then and now is the First United Methodist Church, which relocated in 1953 to the 1100 block of East Silver Springs Boulevard and East Fort King Street. (Kevin M. McCarthy.)

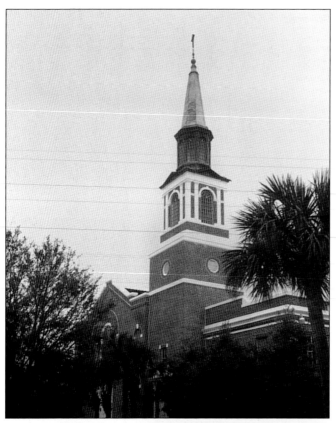

The red-brick building of
First Presbyterian Church
at 511 Southeast Third
Street was completed in the
1920s. The Presbyterians
enjoyed close ties with their
neighbor across the street,
the First Baptist Church.
The 1991 fire that destroyed
its buildings saddened
the Presbyterians as well
as other religious groups.
(Kevin M. McCarthy.)

Grace Episcopal Church
at 503 Southeast Broadway
Street has one of the oldest
church buildings in Ocala.
The church has been in the
same location for almost 100
years. (Kevin M. McCarthy.)

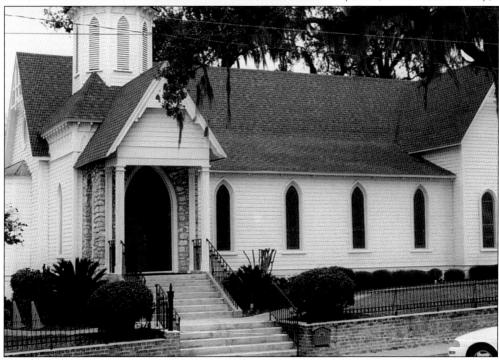

Attorney Robert A. Burford, who wanted a spacious home, built Burford House, located in the 900 block of Southeast Fort King Street in the 1890s. Even his iron fence is unique, having been used around the Courthouse. The house has been restored, and a number of attorneys have used the property for their offices. (Kevin M. McCarthy.)

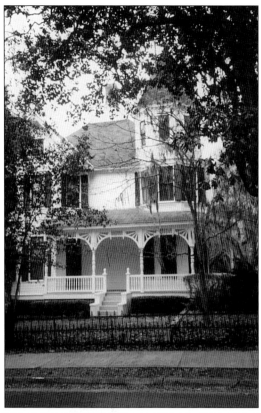

The Edwards Home is one of the most distinctive in Ocala. Since John Edwards built his Richardson Romanesque/Queen Anne mansion around 1909, one can only guess how many people have been stunned seeing this home in a Florida setting. The 7,000-square-foot home occupies the corner of Southeast Wenona Avenue and Southeast Fifth Street. Miss Ava Lee Edwards, an educator, resided there for decades; the home has been remodeled by a member of the Edwards family. (Kevin M. McCarthy.)

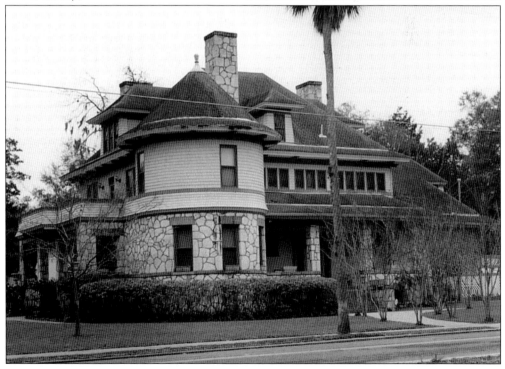

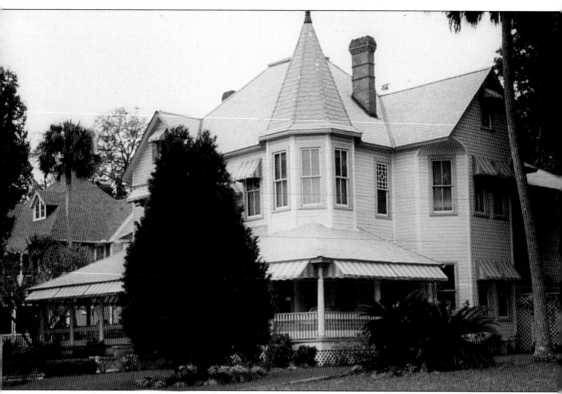

Seven Sisters Inn is a Queen Anne–style Victorian house at 820 Southeast Fort King Street that was built in 1888 in the heart of the historic district. Today, the restoration project is owned by two airline pilots, Bonnie and Ken Oden, who evidently are committed to furnishing American and international experiences to their guests. National honors for the bed and breakfast have poured in, and the Odens have purchased adjoining property. (Kevin M. McCarthy.)

Six

1960s

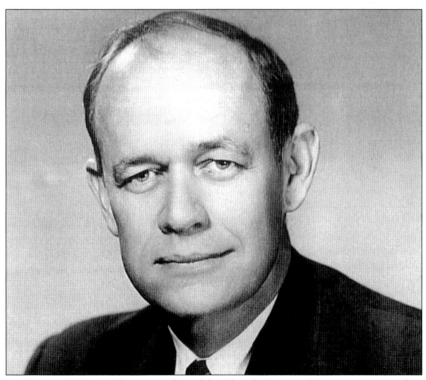

Gov. Farris Bryant (1961–1965) was speaker of the Florida House of Representatives, chairman of the Florida March of Dimes, and, in 1966, became the director of the U.S. Office of Emergency Planning. He had a big impact on roads, and, as an attorney and businessman, he was a leader in the insurance industry. Often joining Bryant at local restaurants like the Big D and The Brahma were Speaker of the Florida House of Representatives Bill Chappell, State Senator L.K. Edwards (a top chop of the Porkchop Gang), Florida Attorney General Jim Kynes, and others with much clout. Locals were pleased with the way that Bryant took care of Ocala/Marion County. (Farris Bryant.)

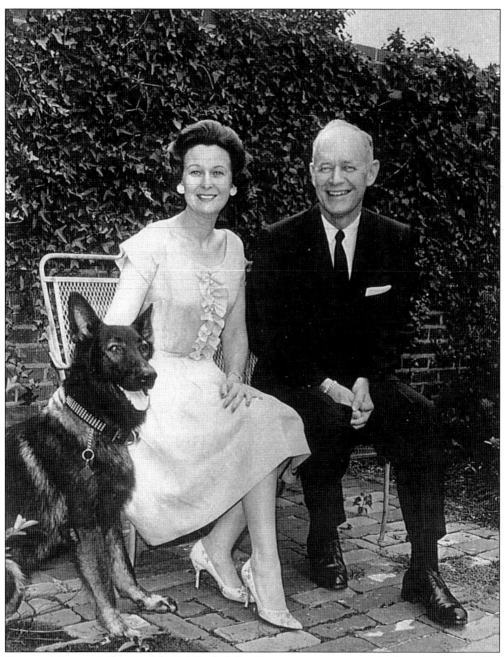

Governor Bryant is shown with First Lady Julia. Bryant, an accountant in the state comptroller office in Tallahassee, met Julia Burnett on a tennis court in 1940. He proposed the next day to the teacher, who grew up in Madison, and they were married in September. Later in Ocala, he built her a big home, which Ocalans thought was grand. She did the landscaping. In the Governor's Mansion in Tallahassee, the First Lady was a gracious hostess, as many Ocalans knew from their visits. (Farris Bryant.)

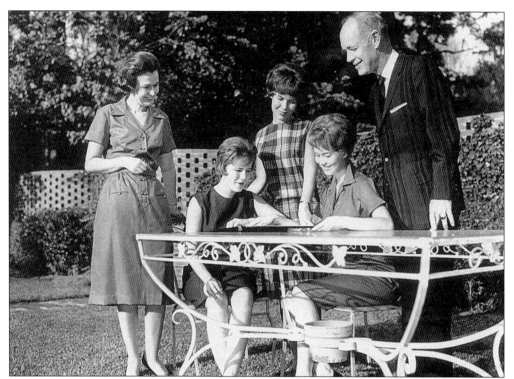

Above are Governor Bryant, the First Lady, and their children. In 1961 when this picture was taken, Julie was 19, Cecilia 14, and Adair 10. Each child earned her place in the sun as the Governor and First Lady vigorously guarded their privacy. (Farris Bryant.)

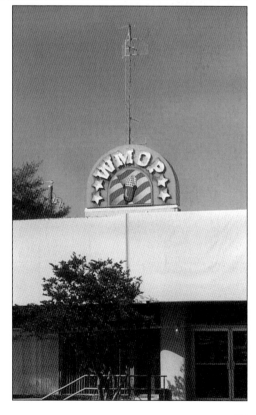

WMOP, owned by Jim Kirk, was a pioneer, country music radio station that stressed the news, weather, and public service announcements. The All-America theme was a big factor with the station, and before the rooster crowed, Country Jim would hum and strum his guitar prior to introducing County Agent Edsel Rowan, who would give updates for his farm friends. During the turbulent 1960s, "Mighty Mop" was a voice of reason, and Chief of Police Kenneth Alvarez and his staff frequently were on the air. As a result of the radio presence of Chief Alvarez, Mayor Kirk, William Jackson, and other leaders, Ocala escaped the turmoil that hurt other cities. Today, WMOP is an all-sports radio station, located on North Main Street close to Union Station. (Kevin M. McCarthy.)

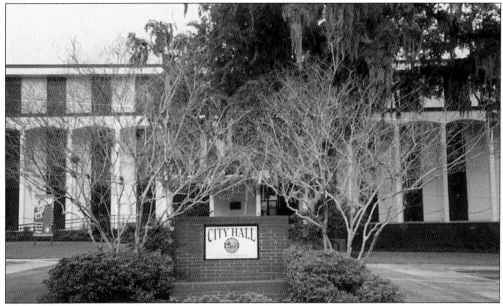

This photograph of City Hall was taken from Southeast Fourth Avenue. East Fort King Street furnishes the northern boundary and Southeast Osceola Avenue, with its railroad tracks, the western boundary. Official city policy is hammered out here by the city council. The mayor has clout, with the city manager being the top administrator with the job of implementing policy for close to 50,000 residents who live in 38.79 square miles. (Kevin M. McCarthy.)

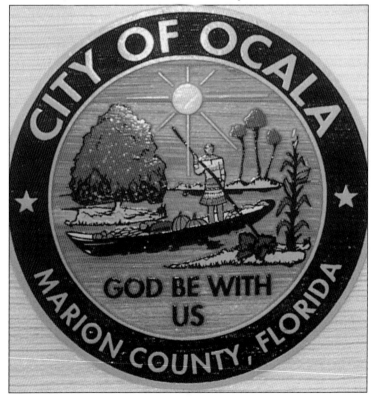

The city seal is loaded with Ocala features: "God Be With Us" (indicating the city's strong churches), a body of water, a Native American, oranges and other agricultural products, trees, and the sun (Kingdom of the Sun is it!). (Kevin M. McCarthy.)

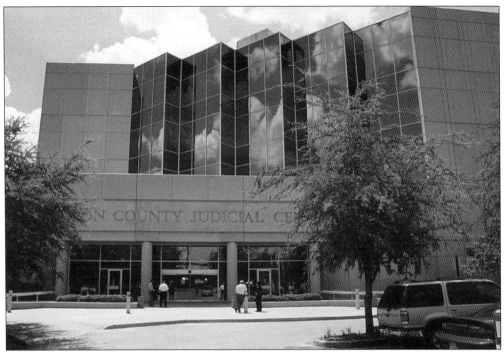

Marion County Judicial Center is shown above at the east entrance. The Marion County Courthouse is in the background, and the buildings are north of West Silver Springs Boulevard and east of Pine Avenue (U.S. 27, 301, 441). (Jay McKenzie.)

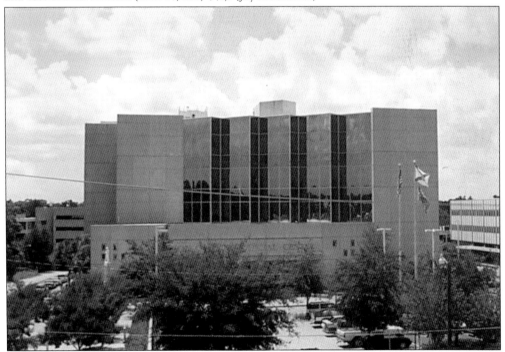

Looking to the west, one can see the Marion County Courthouse (Marion County Judicial Center in front). (Jay McKenzie.)

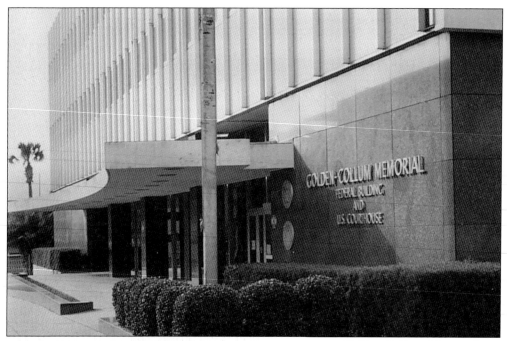

Golden-Collum Memorial Federal Building and the Courthouse are pictured above. (Kevin M. McCarthy.)

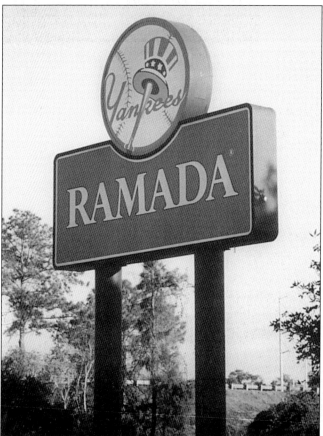

George Steinbrenner owns the Ramada Inn pictured here. Passing motorists on I-75 and U.S. 27 can see the New York Yankees baseball on top of the Ramada sign. Steinbrenner has additional big investments on I-75, one of the busiest roads in the world. (Kevin M. McCarthy.)

Kenneth Williams, president of Central Florida Junior College, departed in early 1960 to become the founding president of Miami-Dade Junior College. Florida Atlantic University was his next stop. He was founding president of three colleges—a U.S. record. (Central Florida Community College.)

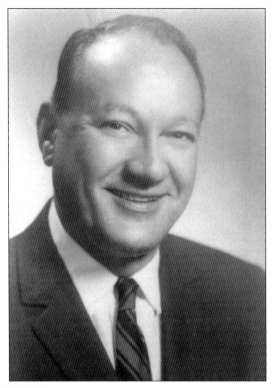

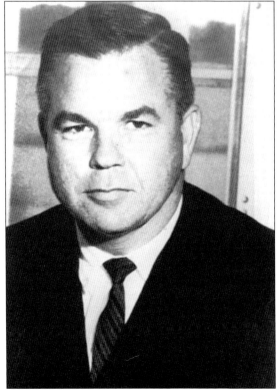

Joseph Fordyce was president of Central Florida Junior College (1960–1966), Santa Fe Junior College (founding president), St. Louis Missouri Community College District, and the American Association of Community and Junior Colleges. Also, he served as vice president of Nova University. (Central Florida Community College.)

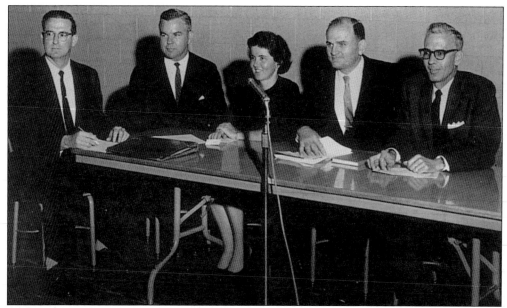

Quality education was a burning issue in the 1960s, and there were many involved in the effort to get all Marion County schools accredited by the Southern Association of Colleges and Schools. The Political Union of Central Florida Junior College organized a panel on "The Relationship of Education and Politics" and hosted the dinner at the College Park Elementary School. From left to right are moderator Ernest Jernigan, chairman, Social Sciences Division, CFJC; Joseph Fordyce, president of CFJC; Bea Atkinson, Marion County Education Association leader; Ollie Daugherty, Marion County director of instruction; and Bill O'Neill, state representative. (Central Florida Community College.)

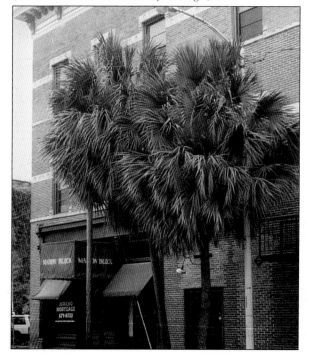

In 1890, Populists held their national convention at the Marion Block Building (which reads "est. 1885" on its side) on Broadway across from the Downtown Square. They put forth anti-monopolistic proposals that were called the "Ocala Demands," which were later, in part, endorsed by the two main political parties: Democratic and Republican. (Kevin M. McCarthy.)

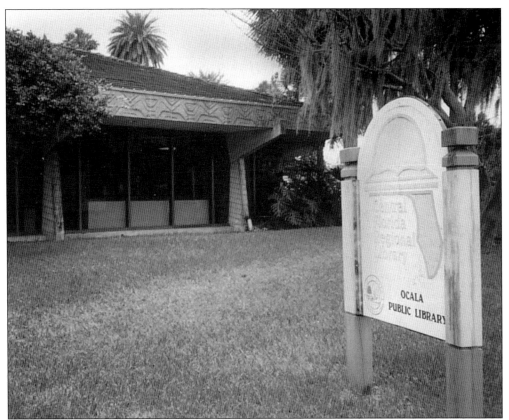

Ocala Public Library has steadily increased its scope to address the needs of a very diverse group of people of all ages and conditions, and it is outgrowing its facilities, which are located at the heart of Ocala—Southeast Osceola Avenue, East Silver Springs Boulevard, and East Fort King Street. (Kevin M. McCarthy.)

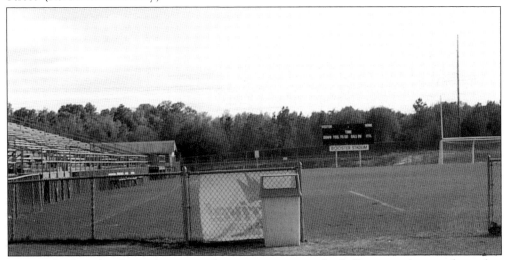

Booster Stadium has been the scene of numerous exciting football games. Among those that have played on the field are Duante Culpepper, Scot Brantley, Tyrone Young, and many other outstanding college and professional players. College scouts abound. (Kevin M. McCarthy.)

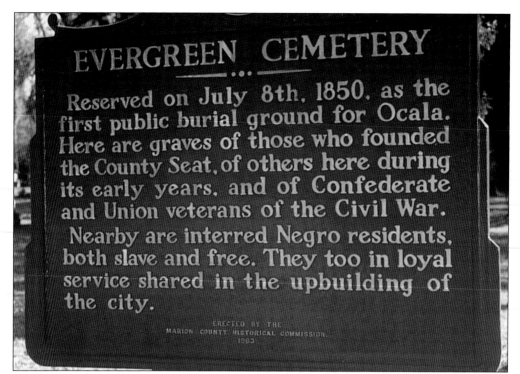

EVERGREEN CEMETERY

Reserved on July 8th, 1850, as the first public burial ground for Ocala. Here are graves of those who founded the County Seat, of others here during its early years, and of Confederate and Union veterans of the Civil War.

Nearby are interred Negro residents, both slave and free. They too in loyal service shared in the upbuilding of the city.

ERECTED BY THE
MARION COUNTY HISTORICAL COMMISSION
1963

Evergreen Cemetery was the first public burial ground for pioneer Ocalans. The Marion County Historical Commission erected the marker in 1963, and the cemetery is south of Northwest Seventh Street between North Pine Avenue and North Magnolia Avenue. (Kevin M. McCarthy.)

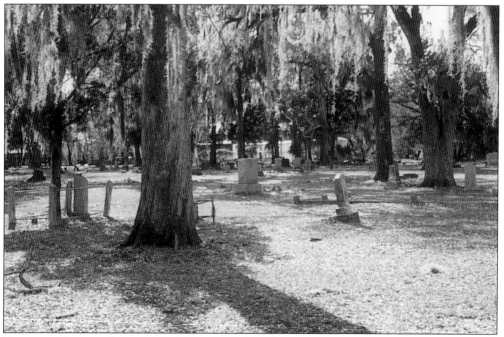

Evergreen Cemetery has many oaks that provide welcome shade. (Kevin M. McCarthy.)

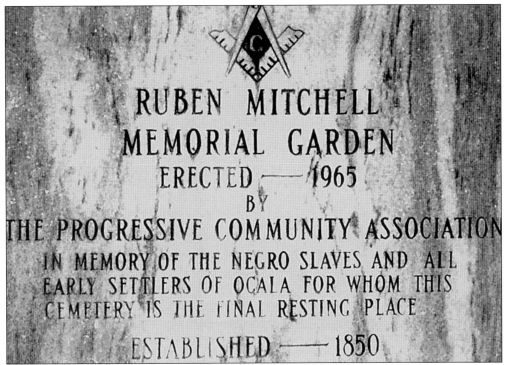

RUBEN MITCHELL
MEMORIAL GARDEN
ERECTED —— 1965
BY
THE PROGRESSIVE COMMUNITY ASSOCIATION
IN MEMORY OF THE NEGRO SLAVES AND ALL
EARLY SETTLERS OF OCALA FOR WHOM THIS
CEMETERY IS THE FINAL RESTING PLACE
ESTABLISHED —— 1850

The Progressive Community Association in memory of African-American slaves and all early settlers of Ocala for whom this cemetery is the final resting place erected Ruben Mitchell Memorial Garden, which is close to Evergreen Cemetery, in 1965. The cemetery was established in 1850. (Kevin M. McCarthy.)

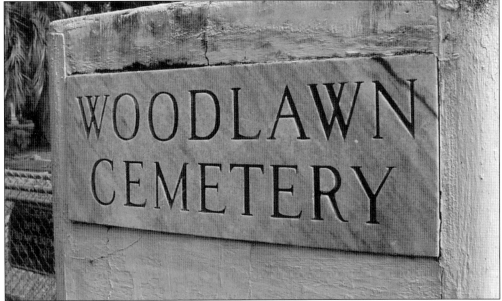

Woodlawn Cemetery, which is city owned, lies north of Northeast Third Street and contains many family plots of citizens who contributed much to the area and bear names such as Dosh, Melton, O'Neal, and Perry, among others. (Jay McKenzie.)

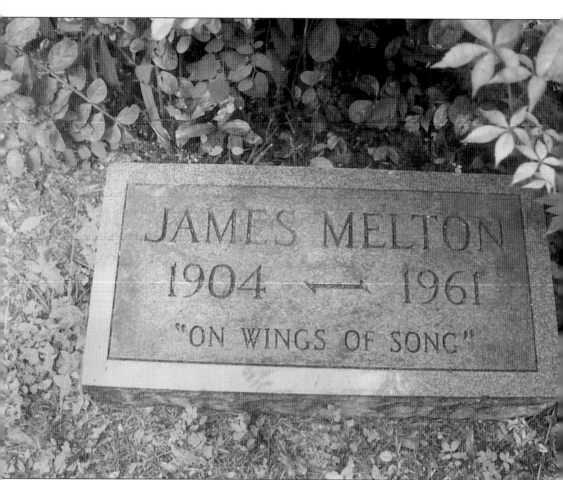

James Melton's gravesite in Woodlawn Cemetery is pictured above. A graduate of Ocala High School, he quickly earned fame and fortune in the 1920s as one of the most respected tenors in the world. He could be heard on the radio and seen in movies. Melton also collected classic cars and became an antique-car attraction owner. (Jay McKenzie.)

Seven

1970s

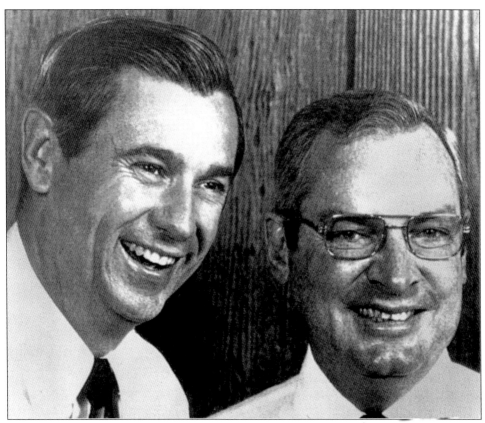

Gov. Reubin Askew (left) is shown with Lt. Gov. Jim Williams. Together the two men made a strong team (1975–1979), and Askew felt free to travel the States and world, promoting goods produced in Florida. Williams, a graduate of Ocala High School with a lifetime of involvement in citrus, cattle, and limerock, served as U.S. deputy secretary of agriculture (1979–1981) and later president of the National Lime Rock Institute before returning to Ocala. (Lou Williams.)

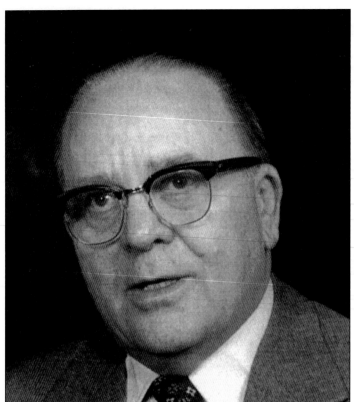

William Butscher, M.D.—a driving force for medical advancement—taught at five medical schools (including the University of Florida Teaching Hospital), earned the Florida Medical Association award for the Doctor of the Year in 1980, and won his suit to force tax assessors to do their job, thus helping education greatly in Marion County and Florida. As a result of his suit filed by attorney Bill O'Neill, many schools got accreditation from the Southern Association of Colleges and Schools. (Jim Butscher.)

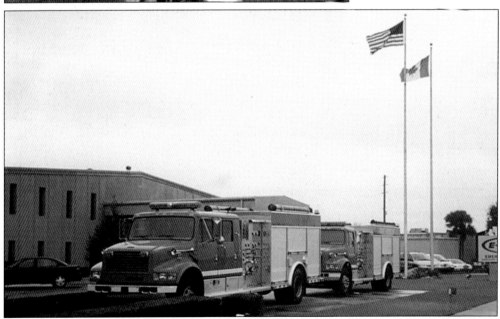

Emergency One was founded in 1974 by Bob Wormser in his garage and quickly grew to become one of the leading manufacturers of emergency vehicles in the world. Measured by the number of employees, E-1 is the top business in Marion County. The main office building is located east of I-75 and north of Airport Road. (Kevin M. McCarthy.)

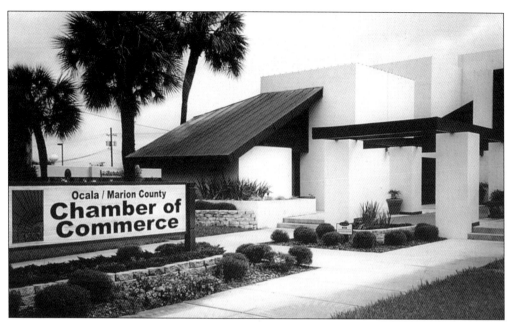

Ocala/Marion County Chamber of Commerce is located where the Ocala House Hotel once stood. It is across from the Downtown Square and between Main and Osceola with Silver Springs Boulevard the boundary to the north. Broadway marks the street to the south. (Kevin M. McCarthy.)

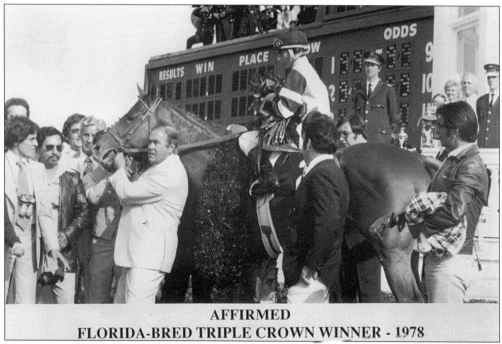

AFFIRMED
FLORIDA-BRED TRIPLE CROWN WINNER - 1978

Affirmed, the horse pictured above, won the Triple Crown in 1978 and was the last horse to accomplish this feat. What great horses like Needles and Carry-Back could not do, this super athlete of Harbor View Farm born in Ocala in 1975 did, defeating the superb Alydar in epic head-to-head duels. (Ocala/Marion County Chamber.)

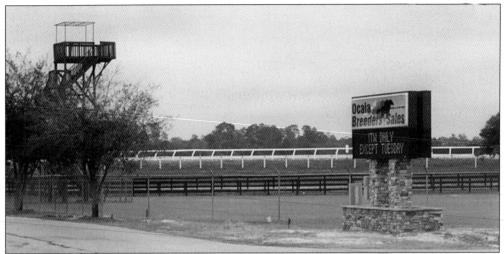

Ocala Breeders' Sales (OBS) is an important center for the sale of promising young horses, and buyers come from around the world; in fact, some land their planes across the street (Southwest Sixtieth Avenue) at Ocala International Airport. In 2000, Ocala Jai-Alai was sold to a subsidiary of OBS. (Kevin M. McCarthy.)

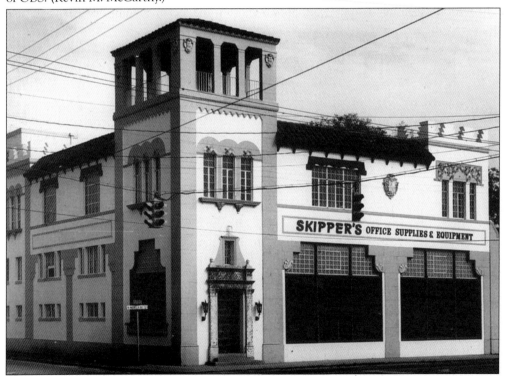

Coca-Cola Bottling Plant earned its space on the Register of Historical Places with its distinctive and beautiful building. In the 1970s David Lee Skipper, who restored the building for the sale of office supplies and equipment, purchased it. The tower, overlooking the busy intersection of North Magnolia Avenue and Northeast Tenth Street, has its own striking story. In the latter part of the 19th century, Ocala was a big market for the Atlanta-based business. (David Lee Skipper.)

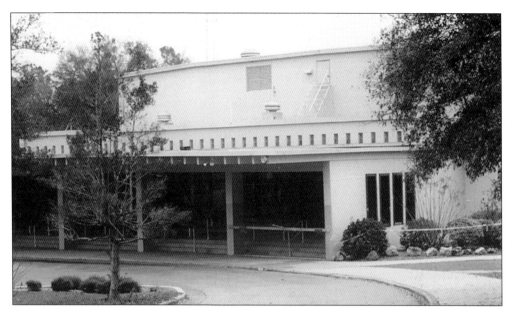

Forest High School and Vanguard High School opened in the early 1970s when Ocala High School was divided into two districts. Shown above is the fourth building occupied by Ocala High School—now Forest High School, which is located at 1614 Southeast Fort King Street across from Downtown Baptist Church, which bought the Mount Vernon Lodge. Forest High School will be relocated to a bigger site in the near future. (Kevin M. McCarthy.)

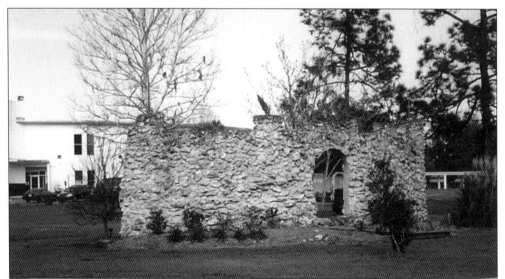

Vanguard High School was established in the early 1970s to assist high school students in the northern part of Ocala. Located just east of North Pine Avenue, its address is 7 Northwest Twenty-eighth Street, and the coquina structure pictured above is located on the school's grounds. Duante Culpepper, all-pro quarterback of the Minnesota Vikings, is the most famous celebrity of Vanguard High School. (Kevin M. McCarthy.)

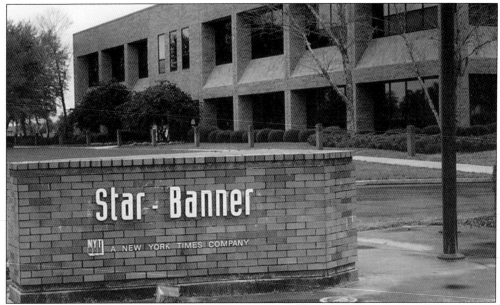

The *Star-Banner* moved into its new building at 2121 Southwest Nineteenth Avenue Road under the leadership of Publisher Paul Brooks. This is its third and final home, according to David Cook. In 1971 the *New York Times* bought the newspaper and, in 1995, dropped the word "Ocala" from the newspaper's name. (Kevin M. McCarthy.)

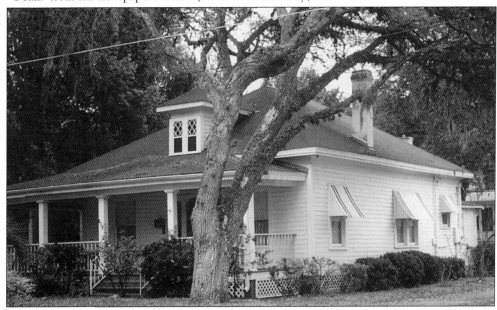

Bert Dosh bought this home at Southeast Fourth Street and Sanchez Avenue and then married Annie Laurie Perry. Their marriage produced four sons—all served with distinction in World War II— and three were graduates of West Point. They also had a daughter. Editor of the *Ocala Star-Banner*, Dosh was president of both the Associated Press of Florida and the Florida Society of Editors and a founding father of Central Florida Community College. The R.N. "Bert" Dosh Bridge of State Road 40 spans the Ocklawaha River. He died in 1970, and the editorial of the *Star-Banner* was titled: "Farewell to Bert Dosh—A Magnificent Person." (Kevin M. McCarthy.)

Eight

1980s

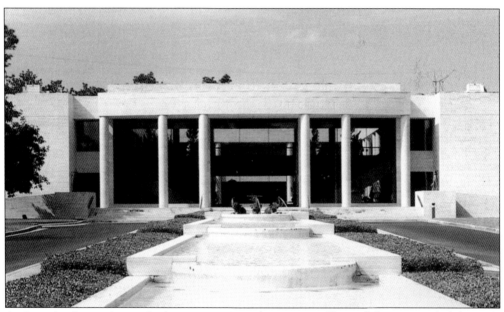

Arthur Appleton, his wife (movie star Martha O'Driscoll), and his sister (Edith-Marie Appleton) provided for a beautiful facility—the Appleton Museum of Art—that would display his remarkable art treasures. The contributions by the Appleton family propelled Ocala in 1987 toward a major-league status in the art world. The Appleton Museum of Art of Florida State University and Central Florida Community College is located at 4333 Northeast Silver Springs Boulevard in a beautiful wooded area. The Appleton Cultural Complex includes Ocala Civic Theatre and Pioneer Garden Club. (Kevin M. McCarthy.)

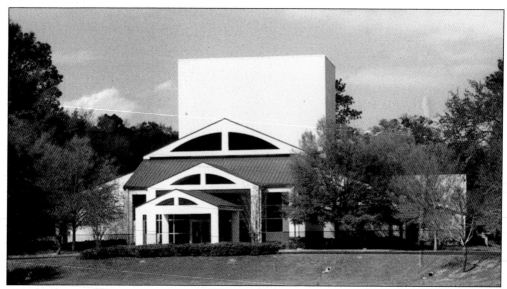

Ocala Civic Theatre (OCT) is extending its scope. Not only does it give youth many opportunities to grow on stage, but the innovative OCT sponsors new dramas such as *Sigsbee*, written by J.T. Glisson and starring Fred Mullen. Part of the Appleton Cultural Complex, the theatre's address is 4337 East Silver Springs Boulevard. (Kevin M. McCarthy.)

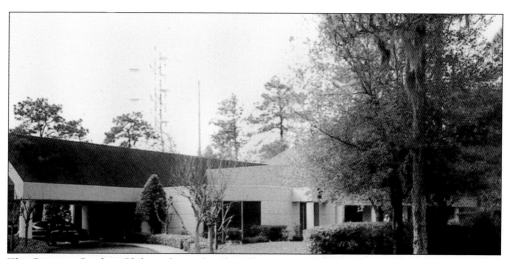

The Pioneer Garden Club, a force that has been around since 1927, owns Pioneer Garden Center in the Appleton Cultural Complex at 4331 East Silver Springs Boulevard. Active in politics, the club is a major reason why Ocala is so green and beautiful. Newcomers to Ocala are pleased to learn that the club is composed of green thumbs willing to share their knowledge; the Horticulture Jamboree furnishes a good example (it's free). (Kevin M. McCarthy.)

In 1988, Cliff Stearns, an Air Force captain, business consultant, advertising executive, owner of motels and restaurants, trustee of Munroe Regional Health Center, was elected to the U.S. House of Representatives and re-elected six times. He schedules town meetings far in advance and is easy to engage in conversation. (Cliff Stearns.)

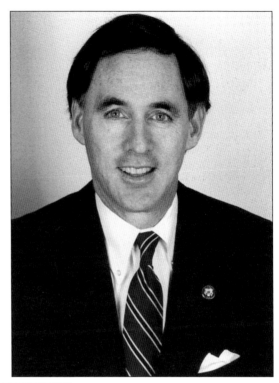

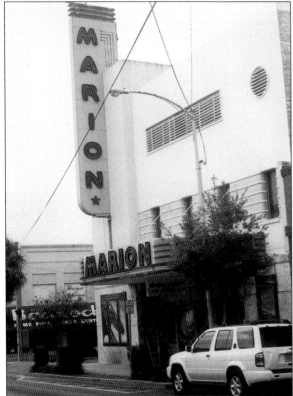

In 1986 Mr. and Mrs. James E. Kirk Jr. gave Marion Theatre, located at 50 Southwest Magnolia Avenue, a block from the Downtown Square, to the City of Ocala. Its distinctive architecture is in the art deco style, and this historic building became Discovery Science Center, much to the delight of countless students. (Kevin M. McCarthy.)

105

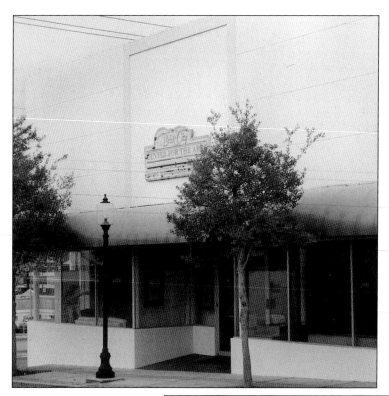

Brick City Center for the Arts offers many programs, one of which is "Bag It at the Brick." For this event, participants bring their lunch to 23 Southwest Broadway Street, a block from Downtown Square, for a delightful cultural experience involving the arts. (Kevin M. McCarthy.)

The Gazebo on the Downtown Square was restored in 1987 under the leadership of the Historic Ocala Preservation Society (HOPS). HOPS was organized in 1981 and has spearheaded the Gazebo program and many others. A number of individuals and businesses donated material, money, and time to restore the Gazebo. (Kevin M. McCarthy.)

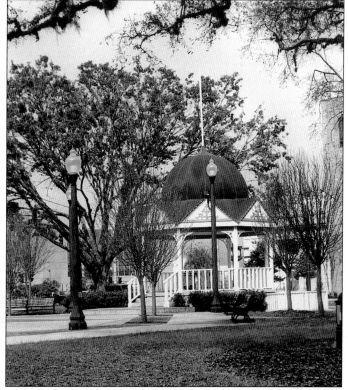

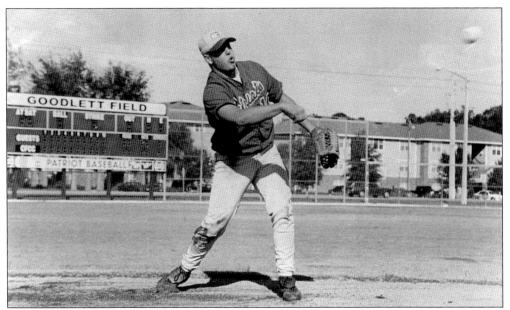

Goodlett Field—named for Henry Goodlett, president (1966–1987) of Central Florida Community College—has seen some splendid baseball over the decades, and at least five Patriots have played in the Major Leagues, according to Vince Murray. Kevin McGlinchy of the Atlanta Braves is probably the most famous player since he pitched two scoreless innings against the New York Yankees in a World Series. Behind the fence is Airport Road. (Central Florida Community College.)

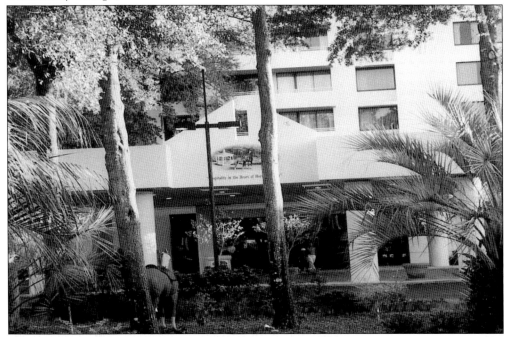

Hilton Ocala, a tall, commanding hotel, occupies 3600 Southwest Thirty-sixth Avenue at the southeast corner of I-75 and State Road 200, and some motorists use the colorful building as a marker on their travels. (Kevin M. McCarthy.)

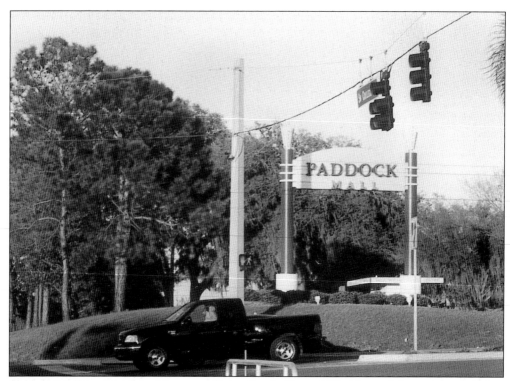

Paddock Mall is one of the biggest malls in North Central Florida, and shoppers come from countless places, judging by their license plates. Built in 1980, the mall is on the east side of State Road 200 (across from Central Florida Community College) and the west side of Southwest Twenty-seventh Avenue. A sizable medical complex and apartment community were built in the immediate vicinity. (Kevin M. McCarthy.)

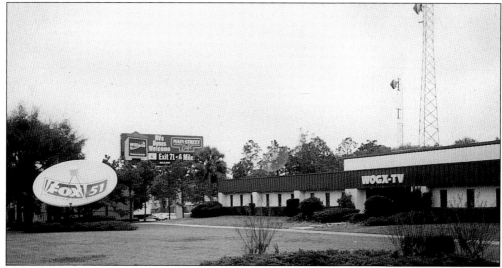

WOGX-TV (FOX 51) is on the east side of I-75 at 1551 Southwest Thirty-seventh Avenue, and Emergency One is a neighbor. (Kevin M. McCarthy.)

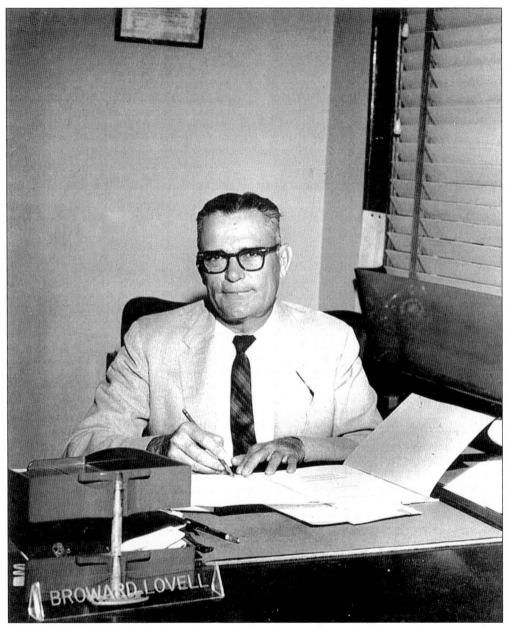

Broward Lovell was a teacher, coach, principal, superintendent of public instruction, president of the Florida Association of Superintendents of Public Instruction, World War II naval officer, college instructor of history and education, dean of adult education, and author of *Gone with the Hickory Stick: School Days in Marion County 1845–1960*. Under his leadership as superintendent, two colleges were founded: Central Florida Junior College and Hampton Junior College. He died in 1988. (Irma Lovell.)

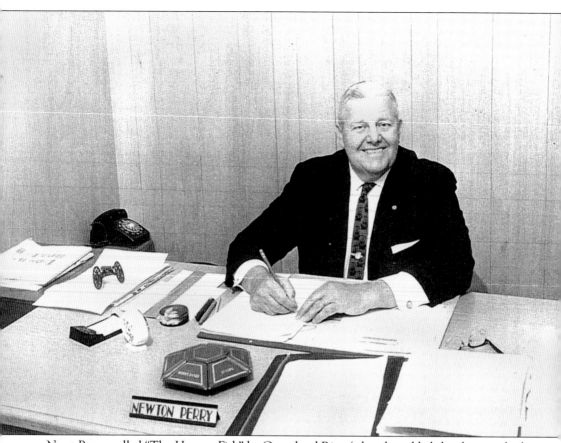

Newt Perry, called "The Human Fish" by Grantland Rice (who also added that he was the best all-around swimmer in America), taught frogmen in World War II for the Navy and mermaids for underwater filming. The innovative underwater pioneer set a world record at Wakulla Springs for deep diving without equipment: 187 feet. As an educator, Perry's career started early. He was one of the best swimming coaches in Florida as a student at Ocala High School, and before he died in 1987, he taught more than 120,000 people to swim. He taught biology and history before serving as principal of the historic Eighth Street Elementary School. The Central Florida Community College pool was named for him. Together with his wife, Dot, one of America's top divers, Newt developed Perry's Swim School at 412 Northeast Seventeenth Avenue in the 1950s. Annually, the Dot Perry Memorial Women's Golf Championship, sponsored by Altrusa, raises much money to promote literacy. Delee Perry, daughter of Newt and Dot and owner of Perry's Swim School, carries on the family tradition and adds to it by hosting parties and weddings in the lovely garden beside the pool. (Newt Perry.)

Nine

1990–2001

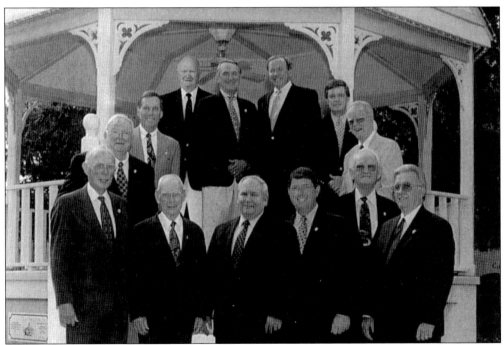

Pictured at the Gazebo on the Downtown Square are mayors, police chiefs, and key leaders who helped Ocala achieve All-America City status in 1995. From left to right are (front row) John Marshall Green, attorney; Kenneth Alvarez, chief; Lee McGehee, chief; Morrey Deen, chief; and E.L. Foster, motel owner; (back row) Jim Kirk, radio station owner; William Swigert, attorney; Doug Oswald, banker; Chris Meffert, attorney; Wayne Rubinas, attorney; Craig Curry, insurance executive; Jack Clark, builder; and Henry Speight, minister. Currently, E.L. Foster is mayor and Morrey Deen, chief. Under the city charter mayors are citizens who serve for low salaries (same for five city councilpersons), and the police chiefs are paid full-time salaries. The Historic Ocala Preservation Society restored the Gazebo. (Ocala Police Department.)

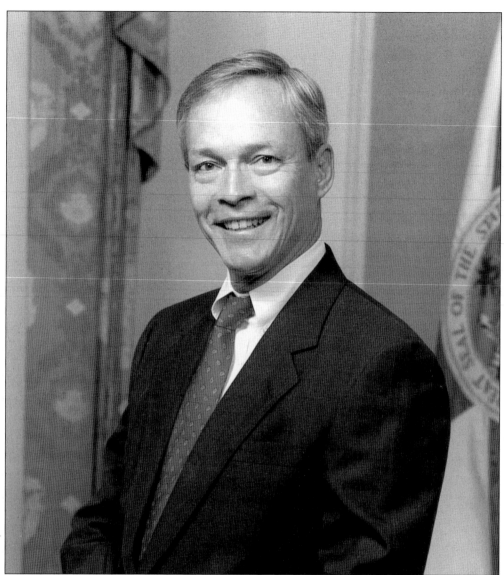

Gov. Kenneth "Buddy" MacKay served in the Air Force as a pilot (captain), earned Most Valuable Legislator awards in both the Florida House of Representatives and Senate, was a member of the Foreign Relations Committee of the U.S. House of Representatives, and, as Florida's lieutenant governor (1991–1998), tackled the toughest bureaucratic problems. In 1999, MacKay, an expert on Latin America, was named special envoy to that region and served in that post until January 20, 2001. The Ocala High School graduate is an attorney and businessman. (Lawton Chiles.)

Karen Thurman, a young math teacher, became councilwoman and mayor of Dunnellon before serving ten years in the Florida Senate. As a senator, she was a strong friend of Central Florida Community College. She was elected to the U.S. House of Representatives in 1992 and re-elected four times. On November 21, 1996, Thurman was named to the powerful House Ways and Means Committee, becoming only the sixth woman to serve on it. At the end of the CFCC summer term in August 2001, she was the commencement speaker. (Karen Thurman.)

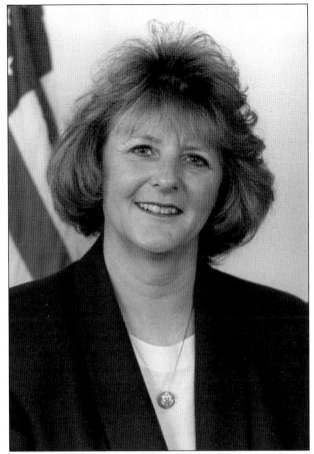

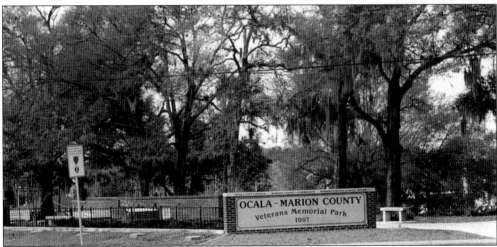

Veterans Memorial Park of Ocala-Marion County was established in 1997 with Tommy Needham (chief fund-raiser and construction superintendent) as the driving force, and the response continues to be very strong. The following words honor one of our best: "S/Sgt Hammett L. Bowen Jr., Congressional Medal of Honor, U.S. Army, 27 June 1969." The park enjoys a superb location: East Fort King Street and S.E. Twenty-fifth Avenue. (Kevin M. McCarthy.)

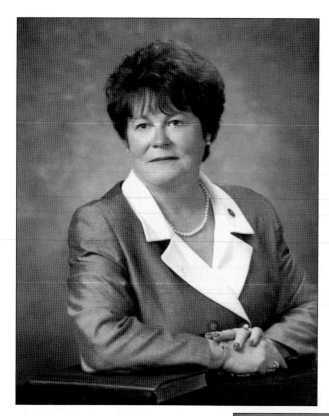

Ocala City Manager Susan Miller, an experienced public administrator, will continue to have much input into the growth of the All-America City. Over the years, Ocala has steadily annexed property, especially when businesses offer to pay their share of costs, and its urban service area is much larger than the 38.79 square miles that is officially Ocala. The job of the city manager is steadily growing. (City of Ocala.)

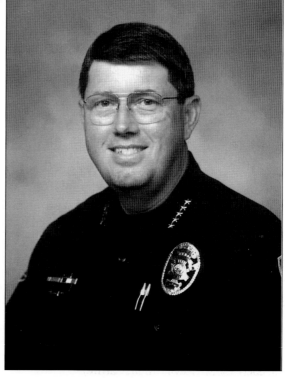

Morrey Deen was appointed chief of police for the Ocala Police Department on February 8, 1995. He is an expert in crime prevention. Since his promotion to chief, homicides total only 20—a low figure for a city of about 50,000 residents. Deen has taught criminal justice courses for CFCC, Rollins College, the International Association of Chiefs of Police, and other organizations; he held the rank of major at the time of retirement from the Military Police (Army Reserves). (Ocala Police Department.)

Mayor E.L. Foster and Chief Morrey Deen were delighted with the crowd of citizens that turned out for the dedication of Ocala Police Department's new headquarters building at 402 South Pine Avenue on December 17, 1999. It contains state-of-the-art computers. (Ocala Police Department.)

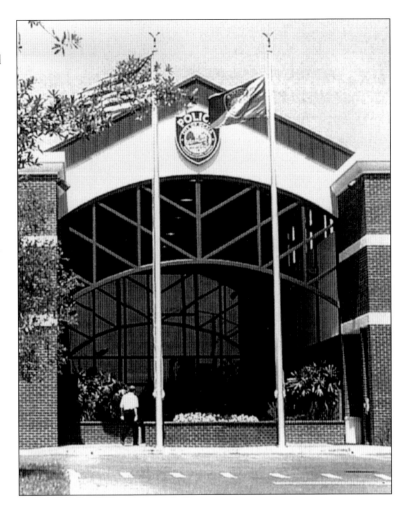

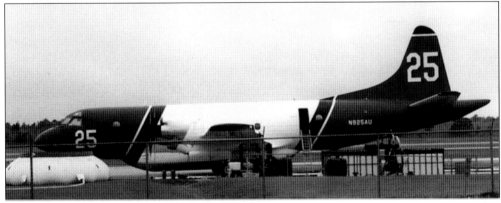

Ocala International Airport (OIA), which is owned and operated by the city, serves many purposes. This P-3 Orion aircraft of the U.S. Forestry Service is being readied for its next mission: fighting wild fires. Ocala's Foreign Trade Zone is yet another purpose, and horse shipments are a common sight at OIA, which is located on Southwest Sixtieth Avenue across from Ocala Breeders' Sales. (Kevin M. McCarthy.)

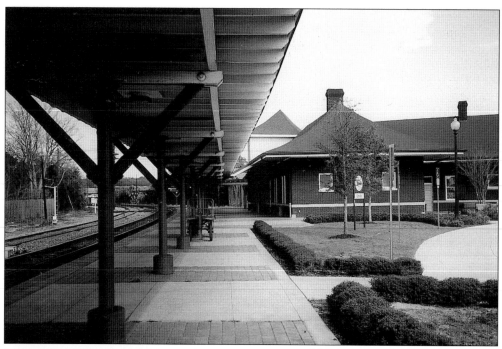

Union Station has been renovated and is, in fact, a transportation complex at 531 Northeast First Avenue used by trains and buses (Greyhound Bus Lines). (Kevin M. McCarthy.)

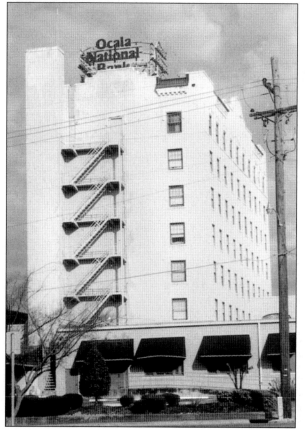

Ocala National Bank, 112 North Magnolia Avenue, has towered over Ocala since 1927, when its building was home to Hotel Marion. In the 1980s, the structure was adapted to an office building and named the Sovereign Building. (Kevin M. McCarthy.)

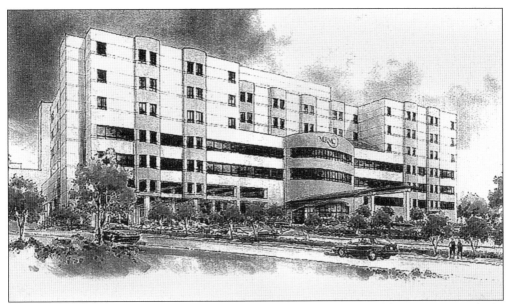

Munroe Regional Medical Center (MRMC) is a community-owned, not-for-profit hospital that dates from 1898. Shown above is the sketch of a new addition to the main campus that will be completed in March 2003. Located at 131 Southwest Fifteenth Street, the hospital is across from Ocala Regional Medical Center (ORMC). Both MRMC and ORMC have earned national honors, and they are expanding in scope and buildings. In the 1950s, many Ocalans went out of town for specialized medical treatment; now, numerous out-of-town patients come to Ocala since a major-league medical complex emerged. (MRMC.)

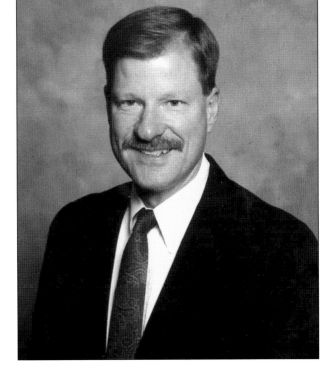

Michael Carmichael, M.D., president of the Ocala Heart Institute, is an internationally respected heart surgeon who, for years, has paid his own way to China to train doctors on the updates concerning heart surgery. The former University of Florida medical college professor is, in reality, a medical missionary. (MRMC.)

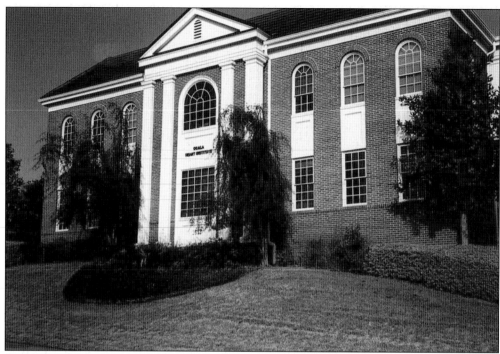

Ocala Heart Institute (OHI) at Munroe Medical Center, a red-brick, white-columned building, is across from MRMC and just south of Ocala Regional Medical Center. Michael Carmichael, president of OHI, said of their mission, "We will be training other cardiovascular surgeons, fellows, and residents in new heart treatments and techniques." (Kevin M. McCarthy.)

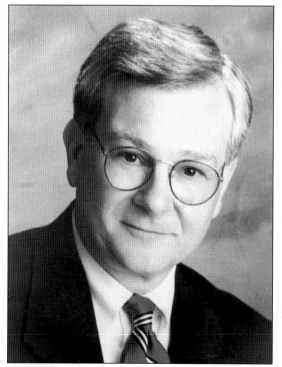

Charles Dassance, president of Central Florida Community College since 1996, is the leader of a comprehensive, multi-campus community college serving more than 8,500 college credit and 15,000 non-credit students. Currently, he is serving a term on the board of directors of the American Association of Community Colleges and is the president of the Florida Association of Colleges and Universities. Dassance, in reality, is president of a higher education complex that, when the University Center is completed in 2002, will have no limits. Active in the community, he holds leadership positions with United Way, Chamber of Commerce, Public Policy Institute, and is quite involved with the Appleton Museum of Art. (CFCC.)

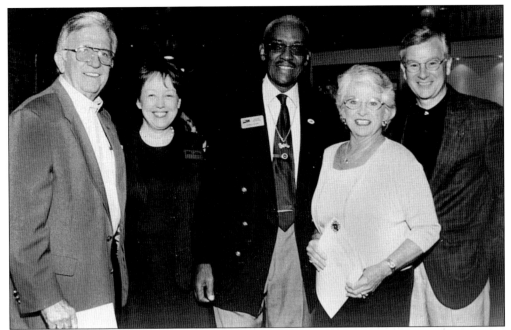

Taste of Ocala, held at Paddock Mall, is Ocala at its best. Ticket buyers get a tremendous choice of tasty food prepared by master chefs who are employed by numerous businesses. It is a festive time to greet old friends and meet new ones while good music is played and give-away drawings abound. Above are some key leaders that raise money for student scholarships at Central Florida Community College. From left to right are Mayor E.L. Foster, Sara Dassance, Chair of Board of Trustees Frank Rasbury, Jo Foster, and President Charles Dassance. (CFCC.)

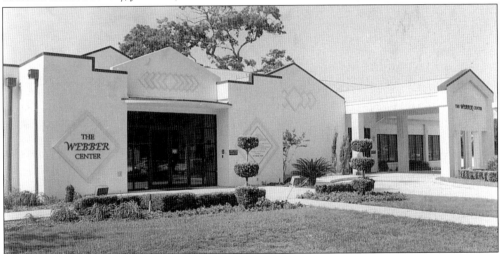

The Webber Center, officially Webber Exhibit and Conference Center, is one of the most beautiful and distinctive buildings on the Central Florida Community College campus. Mrs. Gladys Webber is the benefactor of the center, which is designed to enhance the cultural and learning life of the campus and community. Exhibits have included manatees (a Smithsonian exhibit), trains, and motor sports (with Don Garlits on hand to answer questions). The conference wing was completed in 1999, providing space for conferences and other special events. (CFCC.)

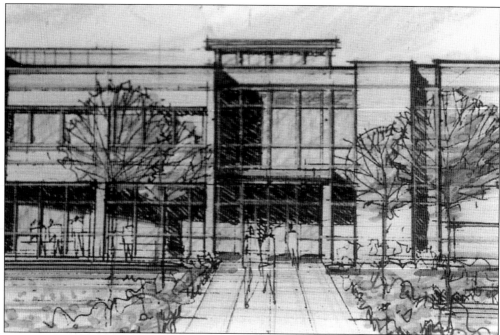

University Center of Central Florida Community College will be operational in 2002. Ocala, in truth, is a university town, and the higher education complex attracts many students who drive a considerable distance. Sprint placed the sketch of the CFCC University Center on the cover of its Ocala-Marion Countywide phone book in March 2001. (CFCC.)

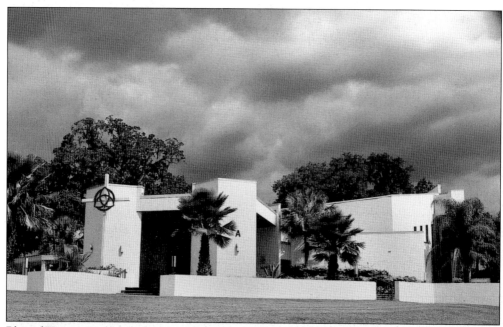

Blessed Trinity Catholic Church, at 5 Southeast Seventeenth Street, seems to have an ongoing building program on its extensive complex. The church sponsors a Greek Festival, which benefits the Trinity Catholic High School and other charities. (Jay McKenzie.)

First Baptist Church begin in 1850 and has grown steadily since then. On October 24, 1991, fire severely damaged its historic buildings on Southeast Third Street, next to First Presbyterian Church. The Associated Press reported the sad news around the world. Church members met on Sundays at Forest High School until they relocated in 1993 to 2801 Southeast Maricamp Road. (Kevin M. McCarthy.)

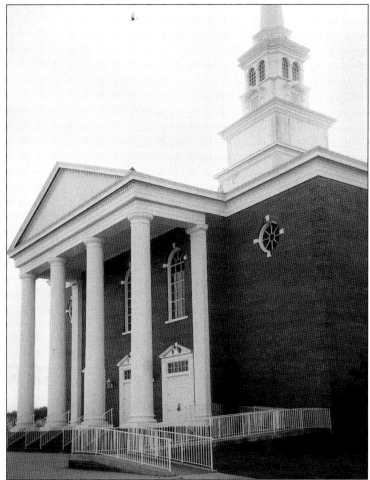

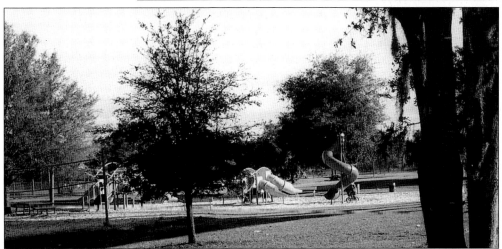

Lillian Bryant Park at 2200 Northwest Seventeenth Place honors a distinguished leader of West Ocala and a longtime educator and administrator. Meetings are held in the building here, and sports can be played by people of all ages. (Kevin M. McCarthy.)

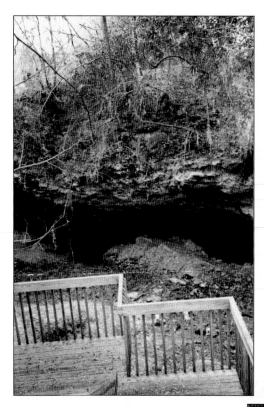

Celebrate 2000 Community Park at Scott Springs was dedicated in 1999 and is located at 2300 Southwest Twenty-fourth Avenue just off Southwest Nineteenth Avenue Road. It has a boardwalk, picnic tables, trails, and grills. The *Star-Banner* vigorously pushed for the city park, and many of its staff physically did much of the work necessary to get the park ready for the public. Native Americans used Scott Springs for centuries, and one can only guess how many times Osceola swam there. (Kevin M. McCarthy.)

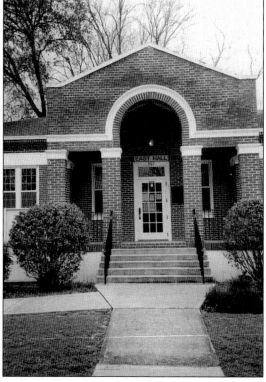

Marion County Museum of History (MCMH) held its opening festivities in 1995. The museum displays invaluable historic pictures and artifacts and hosts the annual Fort King Festival, which draws many from out of town. Located in the McPherson Government Complex at 307 Southeast Twenty-sixth Terrace, it is between Southeast Fort King Street and Southeast Twenty-fifth Avenue. (Kevin M. McCarthy.)

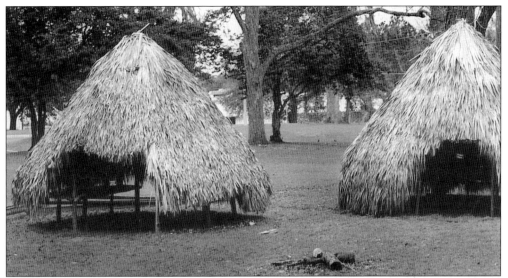

Timucua huts on the grounds of the Marion County Museum of History were built by members of the DeBary family (Earl, Bettie, Jeremy), who have made careful study of Timucua housing, clothing, tools, and agriculture. The Timucua were a remarkable Native American people who lived here before the Seminoles drifted in from Georgia. Native Americans are given full attention at the MCMH. (Kevin M. McCarthy.)

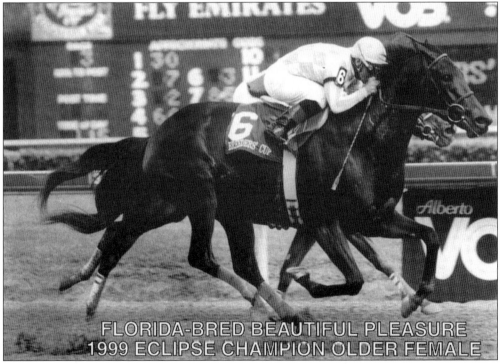

Beautiful Pleasure, bred in Greater Ocala, was the 1999 Eclipse Champion Older Female. A product of Mockingbird Farm, she followed the road to greatness, as did other Ocala-connected horses such as Affirmed, Carry-Back, and Needles. (Ocala/Marion County Chamber of Commerce.)

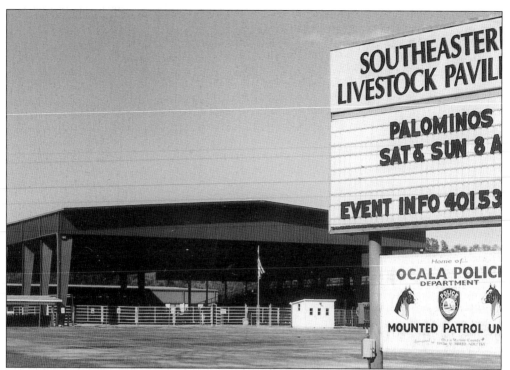

Southeastern Livestock Pavilion, located at 2200 Northeast Jacksonville Road, has been the site of livestock shows, rodeos, religious meetings, and political rallies (Presidential candidate Bill Clinton in 1992 drew a standing-room-only crowd). In addition, the Mounted Patrol Unit of the Ocala Police Department is stationed at the Pavilion. (Kevin M. McCarthy.)

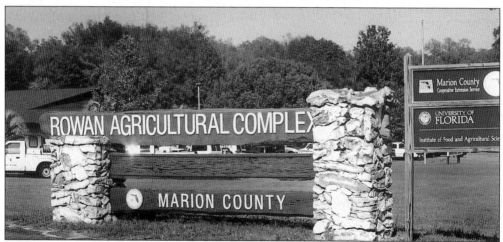

Rowan Agricultural Complex is on Northeast Jacksonville Road next to the Southeastern Livestock Pavilion. The county agent works closely with the University of Florida Institute of Food and Agricultural Sciences, Florida and federal agencies, and agribusiness. The complex is named for County Agent Edsel Rowan, who died in 1995, leaving a legacy of effective work behind. One of the most respected county agents in the United States, he helped all: farm youth, small farmers, and rich horse-farm owners. He earned top awards from local, Florida, and U.S. organizations for his contributions. (Kevin M. McCarthy.)

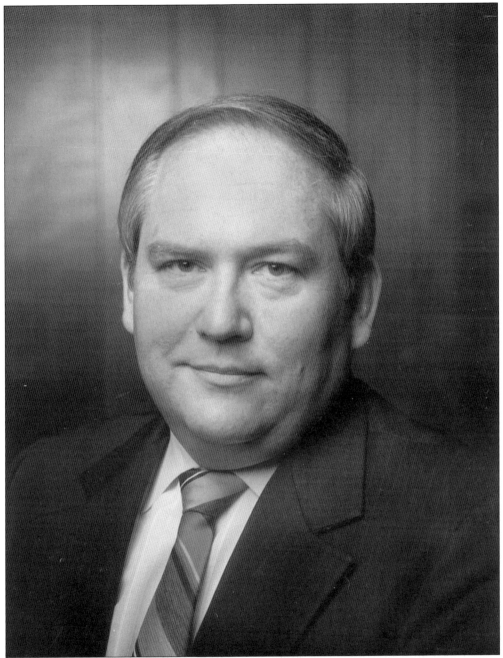

Lee McGehee grew up in law enforcement. His father, F.L. McGehee, was Marion County sheriff, and his uncle, Kenneth Alvarez, chief of the Ocala Police Department (OPD) was a catalyst, with the strong support of Sheriff McGehee, for the establishment of the Criminal Justice Institute of Central Florida Community College. On the cutting edge, Lee McGehee quickly became a leader in both Georgia and Florida before serving as chief of OPD (1974–1995). At his death in 2000, he was director of the Criminal Justice Institute of the Florida Department of Law Enforcement (Tallahassee). As a speaker, one of his favorite topics was the FBI-Barker Shootout (Ma and Fred died) in 1935 at Lake Weir. (Lee McGehee.)

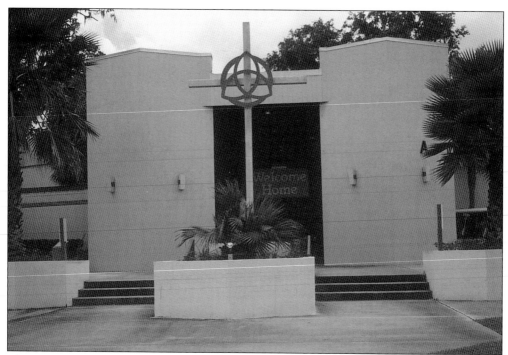

The city's many religious organizations cater to the spiritual needs of Ocalans. (Kevin M. McCarthy.)

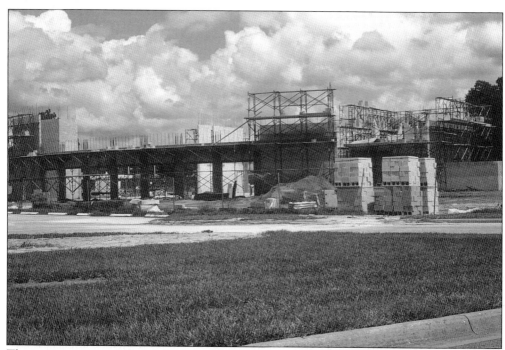

The construction of University Center on the campus of Central Florida Community College represents a strong commitment to the education of everyone in the area. (Kevin M. McCarthy.)

INDEX